World Cultures

Analyzing
Pre-Industrial Societies
In Africa, Asia, Europe,
And the Americas

James T. Shea

Contents

World Cultures

I. INTRODUCTION

It's not easy to condense over ten thousand years of human civilization into a readable overview. I knew that going into this, and I hope this serves as your fair warning as you begin reading this book. I've done my best to both provide a basic understanding of how cultures are built as well as picking interesting, atypical branches of societal development.

My goal is to give you, my reader, both a core understanding of societal development, and a broad toolbox of ideas for developing more specific cultures in your own writing. Think of this book less as a definitive guide to cultures and more as a "tasting menu", exposing you to as many distinct ideas as possible. My goal is to expose you to the breadth of human societies as well as to give you a toolbox of "core ideas" to understand how cultures work.

Before we dive into the actual content, it's important to establish: <u>what is culture</u>, and <u>where does it come from</u>? "Culture" refers to the traits that define groups of people. The concept has its roots in animal behavior; humans sometimes think of themselves as "above" animals, but in many ways human behavior is merely a more complex and organized version of what animals do.

Every animal has a distinct social structure, whether it's a family-based carnivore pack or a larger grazer herd. However, some animals display more intricate patterns worthy of note. Chimpanzees, for example, show many "proto-human" traits such as a tiered society with individual chimpanzees showing deference to those above and contempt for those below. They have even been observed waging at least one "war", an organized long-term effort to destroy an enemy group marked by apparently needless cruelty and aggression.

Humans can build and farm - but so can animals, in their own way. In addition to the construction of complex tunnels and burrows, ants are capable of "farming" aphids. The ants protect the aphids and lead them to plants that the aphids eat. In exchange, the ants eat honeydew that the aphids release; the ants even "milk" the aphids with their antennae in order to force them to release it.

Some animals are capable of distinct language. While all animals "communicate", it was long thought that the nuances and complexities of true language were the realm of humans alone. However, it has been noted that prairie dogs are capable of communicating in a way that implies precise detail; not only simple messages like "danger", but a more complex series of chitters that distinguish details like the nature of the threat, their size, and even their color. Furthermore, the prairie dog language also has regional dialects, deepening its comparison to human language.

Even artistic sense is not limited to humans. Male Bowerbirds, found in New Guinea, attracts mates by making a complex nest of brightly-colored bits and baubles. These nests can be so complex that they even include elements of forced perspective - an element that makes them far more desirable to female Bowerbirds.

Humanity's only apparent "unique" traits involve self-awareness, which leads to concepts like religion and philosophy to try to explain why we're here, what the point is, and so on. Yet even these things are only known because humans are capable of communicating with each other; without access to an animal's inner thoughts, it is impossible to know if they feel the same way. We do know that some animals mourn the dead, including elephants, dolphins, apes and whales. So perhaps even spiritual or philosophical thought could be possible.

Most cultural traditions have their root in a prehistoric, proto-human period. The majority of human history existed in a pre-recording state, which meant that humans transmitted knowledge and information solely through direct contact and memory. Information of any kind was passed down through families and communities, but was not recorded for any form of larger consumption. As a result, we do not know who made the first words, or why they made them that way; our understanding of languages usually begins *in media res* when writing is established, long after the actual origins of the language itself. Knowledge was passed from generation to generation like links in a chain; the process was not always perfect, but in general people maintained the views and traditions of their ancestor. Hence, by the time "prehistory" became "history", humans had been carrying their traditional values for thousands of years.

For this reason it is difficult to talk about the origins of cultural values except in terms of observing instinctual patterns, i.e. protecting one's young, social structures, and so on. Specifics like, for example, why a certain sound is associated with a certain concept linguistically are harder to determine. Specifics like why the deification of thunder has a certain root name that is carried on to many descendant cultures. At some level, a line must be drawn where people say "we don't know". Still, though, those misty origins do eventually coalesce into more observable patterns, and those are what we will be talking about.

World Cultures

II. CULTURAL VALUES

A culture is defined by the ideas it represents and the values it seeks to propagate. Cultures are, in essence, sets of ideas carried from generation to generation. Therefore, in order to discuss cultures, we have to start with what they believe. This is what creates the cultural "core" that all other things - society, art, language, economics, and so on - are built around.

2.1 Idealized Values

"Values" refer to the things that a culture considers important, which informs things like morality, purity, and right-vs-wrong. Values establish the criteria by which all other aspects of a culture are shaped and judged. In that way, they can be considered the most important aspect of cultural discussion.

A concept that is important to understand first and foremost is the *window of discourse*, also known as the Overton window. In short, there is a "core moral set", often described as "centrist", in a given culture. Divergence from that core morality exists, but only to a limited extent. Ideas that exist near the core are seen as normal, and the further you get from the core, the more "unworkable" or "radical" they seem. People will still hold those ideas on some level, but will be shunned by society if they voice them. Any society will have ideas that seem "unthinkable" to them as a whole. However, there will still be an array of what *is* acceptable to them, and people will be relatively free to voice those sentiments without global opposition. All the things we discuss about cultural values and norms exist on a scale. There will be divergences that are acceptable and divergences that are widely rejected. No culture is truly "absolute".

The ways that individuals engage with each other is a reflection of society as a whole - whether they feel able to express themselves openly or if they must guard their feelings behind a constant veneer. In order to reconcile the difference between private feelings and public acceptability, the concept of a social facade is common in most societies. In psychological terms, such behavior is called "masking". In **Japan**, the word *tatemae* is used to describe the "mask" itself. As a form of self-censorship, masking is useful at propagating or controlling societal values. Because only "accepted" values can be safely expressed in public, members of the public are led to believe that everyone in their society holds those core values. Those who deviate from the standard are criticized, socially outcast, or otherwise condemned. In this way, the window of discourse is maintained.

Now that the idea of cultural control is laid out, how do we define what a culture's values *are*? There are some models we can use to narrow it down. The *Inglehart-Welzel cultural map* is a graph that displays countries around the world as points on two axes. The first axis is "traditional" vs "secular-rational" values. The second axis is "survival" vs "self-expression" values. The former has to do with deference to customs and authority, importance of religions, and so on. The second has to do with whether the country is rigidly utilitarian or more open to personal freedom. The map has regional correlation for different parts of the world. For example, the "Confucian" countries (**China**, **Japan** and **South Korea**) are secular-rational combined with survival (although Japan leans more towards self-expression). The "Latin" countries, such as **Mexico**, **Venezuela** and **Brazil**, are solidly traditional, but in the middle ground of survival-vs-self-expression. The "Protestant" countries, such as **Denmark**, **Sweden** and **Norway**, score high in both secular-rational and self-expression.

A limitation of the Inglehart-Welzel format is that it only maps two major issues. However, it does give us a relative starting point for discussion. Cultures are most broadly defined by the values they stand for, as a whole, and the way their societies are shaped exist in conjunction with the pursuit of that core value.

Psychologist Jonathan Haidt conducted tests that led to the development of the *moral foundation theory*. Haidt's research showed that when people of different ideological sets talked about "moral" behavior, they were applying similar reactions to different stimuli. The six stimuli Haidt identified were liberty, fairness, care, loyalty, authority, and sanctity. Self-identified conservatives thought all six were equally important. Liberals and leftists thought that care was more important than all the others, while libertarians polled highest on liberty. All respondents registered strong feelings to their chosen moral values, and all of them identified their feelings as "morality". It is important to understand that when people, or cultures, talk about "moral behavior", they are often talking about very different things that provoke similarly strong emotions.

Empathy is the emotional response of concern and sympathy for other human beings. Discussions of the sanctity of human life and acts of charity are founded in empathy. Almost all ideologies value protecting one's in-group: family, friends and people who share ties with you. Low-empathy ideologies limit their goodwill to these types of people alone, expressing contempt for out-group individuals or perceived "moral degenerates". In modern politics, progressivism is associated with stronger welfare, weaker militaries, and humane treatment of society's undesirables. By contrast, conservative politics are generally more distrustful and aggressive. Conservatives depict progressives as naive and weak; progressives see conservatives as inhumane and hateful.

In **India**, the ancient ruler Ashoka the Great built his empire originally on bloody conquest. However, after the particularly cruel conquest of Kalinga, Ashoka repented and became a Buddhist and a pacifist. His empire mandated not only humanitarian care, but even the welfare of animals. His was an example of a high empathy government (in the standards of the day). In contrast, the Middle Empire of **Assyria** was dominated by cruel punishments and brutal acts of repression even for "good" citizens - who were only considered good as long as they fulfilled their purpose in their aggressive, militaristic society. This is an example of a low empathy government.

Liberty reflects the importance of self-expression and self-determination in a given society. Societies with a low level of liberty value will think that one's own agency is less important than values such as cooperation or obedience. A society based on communal values will curtail the individual's ability to act economically as a way to ensure equality between individuals. Societies with a high level of liberty value will believe that individual expression and action is more important than collective empathy or deference to government.

Note that a love of liberty does not automatically indicate a hatred for slavery; the **Greeks** and **Americans** both built their culture on stated values of freedom, and both allowed slavery because it was the right of individuals to own them. This is a problem with the definition of "liberty" - more freedom for one person can mean less freedom for another. The Greek historian Herodotus described the *Greco-Persian Wars* as wars of freedom (Greece) vs slavery (**Iran**). This was despite the fact that Greece openly practiced slavery, whereas Iran at the time had banned it for all but prisoners of war. Herodotus was talking more about the common person's influence on their government as well as their economic freedom; he described the Iranian citizens as subservient slaves to their imperial overlord. In short, he was only considering the two groups of people that he considered "human", which is to say landed citizens; actual slaves fell below his own considerations in a discussion of freedom.

Tradition is a measure of respect for existing institutions and ideas. It is connected to the concept of things being "sanctified" or "sacred", as well. Respect for a government-in-power often also falls under tradition, since those governments often derive authority from ideological sources. Different cultures will have different ideas of what falls under the veil of "tradition", because in most cases "tradition" is defined by values as well as religion. The concepts here are also noted by automatic, "unreasoned" disgust for violations or breaches. Obviously every society has things that provoke disgust, but some countries are more strict than others.

In ancient **China**, two of the most prominent philosophies were the traditionalist *Ruism* (commonly called *Confucianism*) and the pragmatic *Legalism*. Ruism is defined by obedience to ancestors and moral norms, and has a great number of proper rites and behaviors that show the "proper" levels of respect for one's ancestors and society at large. In contrast, Legalism was a guide for rulership that encouraged a cynical and adaptable approach to leadership. It focused heavily on organization and management, as well as how to get the best results out of one's subordinates. Legalism says that a king should detach himself from his subjects and his own emotions in order to guarantee the best results for his country. Both of these philosophies had egalitarian or meritocratic aspects, but Ruism did so because men of value should be recognized regardless of birth, and Legalism did so because it was the most efficient method. Legalism was the leading philosophy of the short-lived Qin dynasty, while Ruism became a major influence around East Asia when it was adopted by the later Han dynasty.

The nexus of these three concepts is the <u>societal goal</u>. In essence, a society designs itself around a specific set of objectives, and judges the actions of its inhabitants as being beneficial to, or detracting from, that goal. In short, a society arranges itself to support its goal.

For example, *feudal* societies are built around a desire to maintain a certain type of order - the nobles rule and fight, the commoners farm and craft, and the priests maintain the necessary rituals to keep the divine appeased. The goal of a society like this is to preserve itself in that state. Tradition, therefore, takes precedence, while liberty is not valued and is therefore low. Empathy is somewhere in the middle based on the values of the ruling class. *Religious* societies similarly maintain a high tradition, but liberty and empathy depend on the tenets of the religion in question.

A *democratic* society values individual liberty and freedom as good ends in and of themselves. Tradition can range in importance; it is entirely possible for a liberty-focused society to have conservative moral values. Empathy has similar variability; a democratic society can be built on respect for humanity, or it can justify abuse of the weak by the strong as a natural result of the freedom of strong individuals. A *libertarian* society skews high-liberty, low-tradition, and low-empathy for just such a reason.

A *communal* society is based on the idea of restricting personal freedoms and economic mobility in order to ensure that all members of the community are taken care of. As a result, they tend to be medium-to-high empathy (depending on how they view outsiders) alongside low liberty. Tradition is variable depending on the type of commune; some are religious in nature, while Marxist-derived communes are atheist.

A *fascist* society is high-tradition, low-empathy and low-freedom. This is because its goal is to create a self-justifying military machine by appealing to culture clashes. Fascism is centered around a society banding together to stand against out-groups, and by definition, its members must subvert their own independence and well-being in order to support the group. As a result, fascism is the enemy of libertarianism and liberalism (because it takes away freedoms), but also the enemy of empathic ideologies (because it is inhumane and permanently hostile).

2.2 Customs & Traditions

Beyond the core values that define a culture, there are many issues that affect subtler matters. These are traits that affect the ways in which people go about their lives, determining proper behavior and "correct thinking".

Honor is a concept encompassing both personal reputation and morality. Honor exists at some level in almost every society, although the more formal and "tradition-based" a culture is, the more focus there is on it. In **China**, honor is tied in with the concept of *mian*, often translated as "face", which is a measure of social standing, prestige, and due respect. The **Romans** made references to "dignitas" (from which English gets the word *dignity*) and "gravitas" to reference similar concepts - not only one's moral standing, but also how seriously one is taken as a respectable individual.

Honor reflected many parts of a society's values, and was generally used as a measure of compliance with those values. An individual who lived by society's traditions and morality would gain a positive reputation, while a person who eschewed them would gain a negative one. This was both practical and ideological; the practical aspect was the desirability of living and working with someone who held these desired traits, and the ideological aspect was increasing conformity and preferring like individuals.

Honor was not only about individuals, though. The honor of the individual affected the family, past and present. Therefore, maintaining honor was often a communal task; punishing dishonorable individuals before they tainted the family as a whole was perceived as a necessary task. In some societies, a dishonored individual would commit suicide in order to clean the stain from their name. This was especially common in **Japan**, where it was called *seppuku*. Even in modern times, suicide rates are very high in Japan, and it is culturally "tolerated" as a response to dishonor. Suicide amongst students is a noted problem in both Japan and **Korea** (specifically South Korea) due to the high expectations and grueling demands placed upon individuals.

An extreme incarnation of familial honor policing is *honor killing*, found in **Rome**, the **Arab** world, **India**, **China**, the **Mesoamerican** cultures, **Albania** and the **Balkans**. Honor killing was the killing of a family member by other members of the family, incited by dishonorable or shameful actions by the victim. In many cases these kinds of killing were patriarchal in nature, targeting a woman for refusing to participate in an arranged marriage, being the victim of rape, or otherwise deviating from social norms. Men could also be victims for reasons such as homosexuality or even refusing to participate in honor killings themselves. The purpose of honor killings was to maintain the family's status in the community; knowingly abetting dishonor would bring penalties, and redressing the dishonor with violence was often the only way to staunch it.

Politeness is a universal concept across cultures, but as many travelers have experienced, different cultures have different ideas of what's polite and what's impolite. Failing to meet these standards will be seen as rude at best and insulting at worst. Many customs of politeness are relatively minor, but this doesn't mean they're not important. Things like "how to greet someone" or "how to sit at the dinner table" or "how to talk" or "how much personal space to expect" vary from culture to culture, and when people encounter someone with a different idea about those types of things, the experience can be unnerving.

Formality is a common aspect of politeness. How warmly should people treat each other? How familiarly should they behave? Are they allowed to touch each other, and if so, where? How much emotion should they express? In some places, a detached, emotionless performance is considered socially acceptable. In others, a display at that level would be considered cold or unfeeling. The **Chinese** philosophy of *Ruism* was highly formal, with exacting instructions on where people should go and how they should act based on their exact position in society. By contrast, societies such as the **Celts** or **Norse** were more relaxed and boisterous.

<u>Cleanliness</u> refers to traditions and expectations about keeping oneself clean and presentable. The image many have of pre-modern life is a world of unwashed individuals, and while this may have been true in some places, it wasn't universal. Societies that put a great deal of importance on bathing include the **Romans**, who had large public baths, the **Norse**, who bathed at least once a week, and the **Japanese**, who used hot spring baths in addition to rivers or lakes. One of the oldest civilizations, the **Harappan** culture, based its entire city layout around centralized baths and running water. Others include the **Indians**, **Chinese**, **Aztecs**, and **Greeks** (who also had public baths). An alternative to bathing was the *sauna*, which used steam for cleansing purposes. This was used by the **Finns**, the **Koreans** (*hanjeungso*), the **Karo** people of Indonesia (*oukop*), and the "Turkish Bath" used throughout the Muslim world.

Medieval **Europeans** bathed less frequently than their Norse neighbors or Roman predecessors, but there is still documented evidence of regular bathing among medieval peoples, including public bathhouses in 13th century Paris. The decline in bathing (and the rise of the "smelly European" stereotype) came in the 16th century. The practice came under suspicion after the Black Plague; the philosopher Erasmus commented in 1526 that public baths were highly fashionable at the turn of the century, but because of "the new plague", they had been essentially eliminated. Another influencing factor was religious; bath-houses were often host to prostitution and sexual behavior, and were thus seen as (ironically) "unclean" by religious reformers.

Perfumes and other scented items were sometimes an addition to cleanliness, and sometimes a replacement for it. The **Egyptians** made perfumes using plants mixed in oil and cleaned themselves using either *natron* (naturally occurring hydrated soda ash) or *swabu* (a scented soap-paste made from ash or clay). Perfume makers are also recorded in ancient **Mesopotamia** and **India**. In **Rome**, women apparently made common usage of perfumes and other cosmetics; male writers of the period all but unanimously denounced perfumes, with only the poet Ovid expressing any notably positive feelings about it. With the rise of Christianity, perfume became relatively unpopular, but it was preserved in the **Arab** world. With the rise of Islam, perfume became increasingly popular, as cleanliness was an important tenet, and the weekly application of perfume was mandatory if it was available.

Following the crusades, and thus cultural exchange with the Muslim world, the nations of medieval **Europe** began to rediscover perfuming. The first medieval European perfume was made in **Hungary**, and was known as 'Hungary Water" for that reason. After the decline in bathing mentioned earlier, perfume was used to take its place. This continued well into the Industrial era, although ultimately the preference of scents to true hygiene caused many health crises.

Hospitality is an important issue in many cultures. Hospitality may invoke certain rights and expectations both for the host and the guest. The reason for this is often a question of mutual cooperation, or maintaining some sort of neutral ground. In ancient **Greece**, the obligation of good behavior by both host and guest was called *xenia*. In Homer's classic *The Iliad*, one of the reasons that the Trojan War came to pass was because the Trojan prince Paris had violated xenia by kidnapping his host's wife. This was considered an insult to Zeus, king of the gods, because he was the patron of the concept. Xenia shares traits with the **Indian** concept of *atithi devo bhava*, which translates to "the guest is equivalent to God". Both traditions are based on the premise that gods walk among mortals, and all guests (and hosts) should be treated as if they were potentially divine. Among the **Bedouin** peoples, the principle of *diyafa* says that hospitality must be extended, even to enemies, for a certain amount of time. The **Pashtun** people, the majority population of Afghanistan, exhibit a similar principle called *melmastia*. Generosity is seen as a virtue in both cultures, and an opportunity to display it is usually welcomed. In ancient **Irish** culture, hospitality (*oígidecht*) was important for all members of a community, but a particular class, the *briugu*, must go even further. In the legal code *Uraicecht Becc*, the briugu is described as an individual with a certain amount of wealth. A person at this level of wealth received an amount of privilege in society akin to a nobleman, but in exchange they were legally obligated to provide "limitless" hospitality to anyone who asked.

The expectation of <u>generosity</u> can also lead into some more complicated social mores. In **Iran**, the concept of *tarof* is a form of humility that all members of society are expected to engage in. Tarof essentially means being overly indulgent when dealing with another person, with the expectation that the other party will turn down the offer. Here is an example with a host and a guest: the host would be incredibly generous, perhaps more generous than they could afford, with the expectation that the guest will politely turn it down. The pattern repeats itself until the "true intentions" of both parties can be established. This system can be abused if the second party does not turn down the inflated offer, which the first party did not intend to fulfill anyways. Accepting the offer without refusing first is considered impolite. Similar systems exist in other places, such as **Italy** (*fare i complimenti*) and **China**.

<u>Frugality</u> is considered important in many societies, especially poorer ones. Amongst the **Hebrew** peoples, the concept of *bal taschchit* is used to condemn wasteful destruction or resource expenditure. In **Japan**, a similar concept is called *mottainai*, and the word is used as an exclamation to decry wasted material (in a way similar to "what a waste!" in English). In **India**, the phrase *jugaad* is used to describe "frugal innovation", or making useful and functional items out of recycled parts. Jugaad is most commonly expressed in modern India, but some adherents claim the concept is as old as Indian culture. In certain religions, such as the Christian Society of Friends and Puritan sects, frugality is emphasized as a way to ensure that the excess resources will be spent on the poor and needy, rather than wasted on frivolities.

The inverse of frugality is <u>conspicuous consumption</u>. This is a phenomenon where wealth is spent on unnecessary luxuries purely to develop one's image and prestige. While the specific terminology originated out of the *noveau riche* of the Industrial Revolution, the concept exists throughout history. The display of luxury items, fancy clothes and expensive decorations serves as a way to signal one's power and influence. This prestige was referred to as *sign value* by philosopher Jean Baudrillard. In societally important positions, such as nobility or clergy, such displays can be important in order to maintain the proper gravity that the position deserves.

Different religions have different views on material wealth. Christian dogma traditionally identifies the love of wealth, or *Mammon*, as the "root of all evil"; Christ encouraged his followers to give their possessions to the poor, both as a moral act and to show that the rewards of heaven are more important than any earthly luxuries. In Islam, several of Mohammed's wives and followers adopted voluntary poverty in their lives. The *Sufi* sub-sect of Islam follows their example, while mainstream Islam are less concerned with it. Buddhism denounces all material attachments, so the idea of ostentatious displays of wealth goes against its core precepts. In contrast, the Hindu precept of *artha* sees material gain and wealth as a positive nature of existence, alongside virtue and sensual pleasure. It must be supported alongside morality - and greed without morality leads to sin - but wealth is considered positive when the holder is virtuous.

2.3 Gender Identity

Some social standards are dependent on gender and sexual identification. Whether it's the "standard" split of men and women, or a more complicated alternative, most societies have different expectations of people based on their gender.

"Gender" is the set of behaviors primarily, but not necessarily, associated with physical sexual characteristics. This includes both *stereotypes* and *performative behaviors*; the former are assumptions about individuals made based on a culture's ideas of their sex and gender, while the latter are societally-mandated actions that are enforced by ostracism or punishment. For example, a belief that women are emotional is a stereotype, whereas a man being mocked or mistreated for being weak is related to performative behavior. The collection of traits attributed to, and enforced on, gendered individuals are called gender roles.

Many societies were built on a patriarchal model. In such societies, men did everything considered to be of importance or consequence (i.e. earned a living, participated in politics, went to war). Women had a subservient role, limited social mobility, and less control over their own lives. Men, therefore, were expected to be confident and in control, while women were expected to be more meek and obedient. However, there were still variations even within such societies. Among the **Anglo-Saxons**, there were restrictions on women's sexuality and a disregard for their feelings, but at the same time women were able to own property, marry who they wished, and run businesses. However after the invasion of the **Normans**, women in England lost many rights. This was partially because, in Norman society, land ownership was given by lords and kings in exchange for military service. Women were seen as incapable of military service and thus unfit to own land. With their importance reduced, women lost many of their other rights as well. This change illustrates the potential leeway and diversity within a patriarchal model.

In some **European** systems, women were able to inherit noble titles if there were no eligible men in the immediate line of succession. This is called an *agnatic-cognatic* succession system. Some examples of this came from societies where the woman in question would be married, and her husband would control the lands. However, there are cases where the husband would die, and the heiress would regain direct control. This was the case for Matilda of **Tuscany** (1046-1115) as well as Æthelflæd of **Mercia** (870-918), who were both highly influential rulers. In other cases, noblewomen would be granted lands more directly, such as Elvira and Urraca, two of the five children of Ferdinand I of **León**. Although it was rare, women could sometimes lead alongside their husbands; this was true of Joanna of **Flanders** (1295-1374) and Sikelgaita of **Apulia** (1040-1090).

In the society of the **Haudenosaunee**, women were concerned with internal issues (affairs at home, family, and crafting), while men dealt with external ones (hunting, trading and war). While this setup isn't necessarily unique, women were given more power and control in their spheres of influence than many other cultures. Women were considered the "keepers of culture", maintaining and defining the values of the tribe. Women chose the tribal chiefs and monitored them to ensure they fulfilled their role. Women were considered wiser and more practical than men, while men were brought up to be brave and stoic.

For the **Minang** people of Indonesia, landholding is a female right, and land passes from mother to daughter. Women are expected to stay at home, whereas boys have a comparatively more nomadic lifestyle. At age seven, young boys leave the home to study at the nearest *surau*, which is an assembly building and temple used for religious instruction. As a teenager, the boy is told to wander the region, learning from his experiences and returning stronger and more knowledgeable. It is for this reason that women are given land rights, since they stay at home for their entire lives while the men do not.

In the culture of the **Amazigh** (or **Berber**) people of North Africa, men are primarily tasked with handling herding, while women stay at home and make crafts. Both men and women may lead tribes, and gender equality is a strongly ensconced hereditary value. The **Tuareg** people are similarly patterned, with a few additional aspects. Firstly, for the Amazigh, men choose women for marriage - for the Tuaregs, it is the other way around. Secondly, in Tuareg society, it is *men* who are veiled, not women. Historically, this is because the Tuareg men are out in the desert, where face-veiling provides protection against sand and sun, while the women are in the relative safety of home. "Taking the veil" is a rite of passage for the Tuaregs, symbolizing the transition from a boy to a man.

The **Mosuo** people of southern China are an example of a female-driven society. The Mosuo describe themselves as matriarchal; women head households, run businesses, own land and inherit wealth. Men have relatively few duties (mostly farming and fishing), but are consulted with large decisions and hold certain positions of arguable authority. The Mosuo do not marry, but will change between partners as it suits them to do, or even have multiple partners simultaneously without stigma. Even fathership is not considered a particular concern, as the child is raised by the mother's family regardless of whether or not the father's identity is known.

The **Norse** had relatively traditional gender roles in many ways - men fight and control, women keep the homestead. One particular quirk of Norse society was that sorcery and magic (*seidr*) were considered to be in the realm of women. Men could practice magic, but it was stigmatized, and in doing so they made themselves effete (or *ergi*). Sorcery included divination as well as trickery and hexes; sorceress circles were used to connect to the spiritual realm in times of crisis, to ask the gods for guidance. Ironically, the chief god Odin himself was said to be a practitioner of seidr, and in the myths, Loki accused him of being unmanly because of it.

The nomadic **Scythians**, **Sarmatians**, and **Issedones** of central Asia were described by their more civilized contemporaries as possessing egalitarian or matriarchal gender systems. The historians Herodotus and Hippocrates described the Sarmatians as being matriarchal in nature. Unmarried women served as warriors until they'd killed enough foes to earn the right to marry, at which point they would take a sedentary civilian role. Conversely, men were said to be more passive, fulfilling feminine roles in their society. Such observations are coupled with more fantastic observations that may be less true, but it is known that Sarmatian and Scythian women have been found buried with weaponry (the latter more than the former). The Issedones are described only from second-hand accounts; Herodotus provides accounts given to him by Scythians, who describe them as "*observers of justice: and it is to be remarked that their women have equal authority with the men*".

The next gender-related issue concerns <u>authority and family</u>: who gets to be in charge, and whose family connections are more important. For many cultures the answer to both has traditionally been "the man", but this is not universal. Determining who is in charge is a question of *patriarchy* vs *matriarchy*. Determining whose family line is carried down is *patrilineal* vs *matrilineal* descent. In some cases, marriage involves the couple moving near the husband's family (*patrilocal*) or the wife's family (*matrilocal*). These different categories affect the way that cultures think about the family unit and the role of men and women within it.

Several *matriarchal* societies were discussed in the previous section due to the distinct gender roles of those societies. Almost every "matriarchal" society has slightly different gender roles than traditional patriarchal societies do, to reflect the fact that women are expected to run things. There are some societies that have more patriarchal gender roles where, for one reason or another, women are expected to "run things" (usually while the men are away). This includes **Sparta** in Greece and **Manipur** in India.

Matrilineal societies have a more subtle gender difference compared to full-on matriarchies (although some obviously are both). In a matrilineal society, the mother's bloodline is what's important. This grants women a more important role in terms of inheritance and landholding, but does not guarantee them direct control in society (i.e.

lawmaking and self-determination). For example, the **Akan** people of west Africa are ruled by elected male monarchs, the families from which those kings are drawn are matrilineal in nature. It is female descent that determines eligibility to be elected. Similarly, the **Guanches** people of the Canary Islands were ruled by male kings, but those kings were chosen based on a matrilineal connection to a progenitor queen. Some matrilineal societies that have already been discussed include the **Haudenosaunee, Minang, Mosuo** and **Tuareg** peoples. Others include the **Ashanti** of Ghana, the **Soninke** of Mali, the **Nair** of India, the **Karen** of southeast Asia, and the **Navajo** and **Hopi** of the American southwest.

Finally, *matrilocality* is about clan identification and mobility. Like matrilineality, it is often about which part of the family is considered more important. It plays a subtle but important role in family dynamics; the husband is the "outsider", and the wife is the "insider". The daughter is the one who is familiar to the rest of the family, while the husband is the one who must prove themselves and try to fit in. Matrilocal arrangements were most common in societies that also had matriarchal and matrilineal traits.

One common version of this is based on inter-clan or inter-tribe marriage. For the **Haudenosaunee**, if a marriage was arranged between members of two clans, the husband would go to live with the wife's clan. There they would live either in their own household or, if they were too young for that, in the household of the wife's family.

For the **Nair** people, matrilocality was part of a complex matrilineal household arrangement. The Nair household was called a *tharavad*, and it held somewhere between 50 and 200 people. The tharavad was headed by the eldest male, the *karnavan*, who had control over most aspects of the household. However, inheritance was matrilineal, and men of the household who *weren't* the karnavan had lower status than the women of the household. Notably, men connected to the family as husbands were only allowed in the household at night, and were made to leave in the morning. For this reason they usually slept in nearby houses. The exact setup is complex and accounts vary, but it is certain that the household was women-centric despite being headed by a man.

In addition to roles for the two traditional genders, many cultures also have a <u>Third Gender</u> (with a rare fourth as well). This is usually designed for members of one biological sex who wish to fulfill a role outside their traditional associated gender, and plays into expectations of gender behavior just as much as the "standard" two genders.

Many Native American peoples, including the **Cheyenne, Oglala Lakota, Crow** and **Navajo**, have the concept of a *"two-spirit"*. These are individuals who are assigned as either gender at birth but who later adopt a special androgynous role. Within different cultural groups, the two-spirits play different roles. For the **Yuki** people, they are designated as keepers of oral tradition. The Oglala Lakota consider them to have spiritual abilities such as fortune-telling and conferring lucky names on children. The roles and restrictions of a two-spirit depend strongly on the broader gender roles and values of the cultural group. In some groups, true "males" will be humiliated or angered if they are treated as women, but assigned-male-at-birth two-spirits do not suffer any stigma for their own relative femininity.

In **India**, the term *hijra* is used to denote male-to-female transgender people (though the modern community prefers the term *khwaja sira*). Hijras are recognized by the Indian government as a third gender and have a long history in Indian culture, being documented in the *Ramayana*, the *Mahabharata*, and the *Kama Sutra*. Hijras perform special roles related to birth and marriage, although their specific purpose is different in different regions of India.

In the **Balkan** region, *"sworn virgins"* are a rare "female-to-male" transgender identity. In these cases, a woman swears an oath of celibacy in front of tribal elders, after which she is allowed to essentially live as a man. The privileges granted by this act include performative things such as wearing male clothes, using a male name and sitting and talking socially with men. However, it also includes more substantial actions such as taking on male work and acting as the head of one's household (usually when living with female relatives). This means that the act of becoming a sworn virgin is sometimes done for what we would think of as "transgender" reasons (i.e. "I feel like the wrong gender") and sometimes for pragmatic reasons (freedom & independence). In cases where male heirs had died, it was sometimes necessary for a daughter to become a sworn virgin to claim proper inheritance.

A similar rationale existed for the **Nandi** people of east Africa. The Nandi had relatively rare marriages between women where one woman would ceremonially adopt a male role, with all the privileges and expectations that accorded. The newly christened man would be prohibited from having sexual relations with their wife; they instead had to select a stand-in to actually impregnate her. However, children born of the wife would be treated as the husband's children, not the children of the actual biological father, the surrogate.

The peoples of **Polynesia** have differing third-gender roles, such as the *māhū* of **Hawaii**, the *fakaleiti* of **Tonga**, *asog* in the **Philippines**, and the *fa'afafine* of **Samoa**. These examples are assigned-male-at-birth individuals given a more feminine role to fill. In the case of the Samoan fa'afafine, boys who display feminine traits and a preference for "female" tasks such as cleaning will often be recognized as fa'afafine. Such individuals exist between masculine and feminine gender roles, primarily fulfilling feminine roles but able to act as a male in certain circumstances.

In **Ethiopia**, the **Amhara** people of the highlands used the term "*wändarwäräd*", or "male-female", to describe transgender people historically. According to anthropologist Simon Messing, these individuals were treated as "God's mistakes", whose condition was beyond their power to fix and thus tolerated. In the southern region, the **Maale** people had "*ashtime*", who crossed from masculine to feminine roles.

In **Arabic** culture, the term *mukhannathun* ("men who resemble women") is used to describe male crossdressers and male-to-female transgendered people. They are mentioned briefly in the Koran; Mohammed banishes one for their immorality, but does not kill them because they were devout. In general, Mohammed condemned their behavior as immoral; he also condemned women who behaved like men. Later scholars such as Al-Kirmani, Al-Ayni, and Ibn Hajar drew distinctions between men who were "naturally" effeminate (who were blameless) and men who put on artificial airs of femininity. However, Al-Ayni and Ibn Hajar stated that naturally effeminate men must try not to behave in such a way, and if they continued after being warned, they should be condemned. In several modern Muslim countries, such as **Iran** and **Egypt**, gender reassignment surgery is offered freely as an alternative to engaging in homosexuality, which is considered worse.

2.4 Expression of Sexuality

The importance of sex is a constant in human society. Some people have a tendency to see the past as being austere and clinical, but that's not always the case. There's preserved graffiti from Pompeii that's just as graphic, vulgar and frank as the kind of stuff you'd find on a bathroom wall (or online message board) today. In the Epic of Gilgamesh, one of mankind's oldest recorded stories, sexual intercourse (with a priestess of a sex goddess, no less) is used to turn a wild man "civilized". Sexual mores of all kinds and configurations can be found throughout human history.

It comes to a surprise to some people to find out how common homosexuality and bisexuality were in the ancient world. With the stigma instituted by the *Abrahamic* religions (*Judaism, Christianity* and *Islam*), it's easy to forget that a majority of Europe in ancient times were incredibly open and accepting about homosexual acts. Although in general it is important to note that these "homosexual acts" were more akin to a form of pervasive bisexuality. "Exclusivity" was rare (declarations of both "men only" and "women only" were found on the walls at Pompeii), but the core concept of limiting oneself to a single sex was apparently unusual and worth noting.

Not all homosexuality was treated equally. The **Romans**, for example, were very fond of homosexuality where a superior dominates an inferior, but openly contemptuous of the reverse. It was considered shameful to be penetrated, and this particular accusation dogged Julius Caesar himself for years (his assumed lover was King Nicomedes IV of Bithynia, adding a political layer as well). A similar value set was used by the **Assyrians**, who thought it praiseworthy and beneficial to penetrate, but shameful to be penetrated. The **Norse** took this a step further, suggesting that homosexuality was acceptable only as rape (i.e. to humiliate a defeated enemy) - but in this form, it was relatively common. Similarly, the Romans indicated that rape-after-defeat was a common fear for both men and women, whether in wartime or as the result of banditry.

One form of this "aggressive homosexuality" mindset common throughout the world was the pairing of an older man with a young boy. This was practiced by the Romans, the **Greeks** (*paiderastia*), the **Japanese** (*shudo*), the **Iranians** (*bacha bazi*) and the **Mayans** (motivated by the god Chin), along with many other smaller cultures such as the **Siwan** people of western Egypt or the **Keraki** of Oceania. In addition to sex, such relationships also tended to have a "grooming" component, where the older male would lavish favors and niceties upon the younger.

However, more equal forms of homosexuality can be found throughout the world, as well. An ancient law code of the **Hittite** peoples outlaws incest (including father-son), but makes no proscription on any other form of homosexuality, suggesting that it was at least accepted. Homosexual relationships were documented among the **Celts** by historians of the age. Diodorus Siculus recorded this: "*Although their wives are comely, they have very little to do with them, but rage with lust, in outlandish fashion, for the embraces of males.*" Most sources of the time suggested that such relationships were relatively casual and free, without any sort of superior-inferior relationship. Among the **Harari** and **Kemant** people of Ethiopia, male homosexuality has been documented in both adult-paired and pedagogic relationships.

Female homosexuality tends to be mostly equal, but is rarer. Ford & Beach's "Patterns of Sexual Behavior" identifies it amongst the **Aranda** of Australia and the **Mbundu**, **Nama**, **Azande** and **Dahomeans** of Africa. As an exception, the historian Plutarch alleged that the women of **Sparta** forged pedagogic lesbian relationships similar to those forged by Greek men.

Each society has its own views about <u>sexual openness</u>, whether homosexually or heterosexually. Furthermore, this ties into views about monogamy versus "open relationships": whether sex was something sacred between two linked partners, or something more akin to a passing fancy. As with homosexuality, the spread of the Abrahamic religions standardized a contempt for extra-marital sex and adultery that was not always present before it.

In ancient **Egypt**, adultery was considered a serious crime. However, there was no judgment about pre-marital sex, meaning that unmarried men and women could engage in sex as they pleased without stigma. Marriage itself was more an issue of property sharing than sacred bonds; divorce was feasible, but complicated in terms of who got what.

In the mythic **Gaelic** story of *Cu Chulainn,* the titular hero is married to Emer, whose hand he won in a complex game of riddles. However, he has many affairs outside of their marriage that she does not seem to mind (apart from one example that is notable as her "only jealousy"). The reverse is also true, with Cu Chulainn's archnemesis Queen Medb telling her husband that she intends to have many lovers outside their marriage, which he accepts. This, along with the accounts of contemporaries, suggests that monogamy is not as important to Celtic culture as it is to others. The historian Siculus stated that young **Celtic** men would offer themselves sexually and openly to visitors, and be offended if their advances were rebuffed.

A comparison was made between the Celtic open views and **Roman** "closed" views on sexuality, as reported by Cassius Dio: "*a very witty remark is reported to have been made by the wife of Argentocoxus, a Caledonian, to Julia Augusta. When the empress was jesting with her, after the treaty, about the free intercourse of her sex with men in Britain, she replied: "We fulfil the demands of nature in a much better way than do you Roman women; for we consort openly with the best men, whereas you let yourselves be debauched in secret by the vilest.""*

In contrast with the Celts, the **Germanic** peoples were recorded by Tacitus as being monogamous. In this regard he stated that they were "*almost alone among barbarians*", which gives us contextual clues about open relationships in other cultures of the ancient world. Adultery was also punished severely, bearing a heavy stigma for both men and women.

The **Mosuo** people, described earlier in this chapter, have open relationships with no particular attachment behind them. These "walking marriages" are based on mutual attraction, which leads to the man visiting the woman at night and then leaving in the morning. There is no "slut shaming" for men or women; either may have as many partners as they wish, although many do settle with only one at a time. The child is always raised among the mother's household; the father is respected for his contribution, so to speak, but his role in the child's life is relatively small, and if the father is not known it is not a source of major stigma.

According to Ford & Beach's *Patterns of Sexual Behavior*, the Oceanic **Trobianders** and **Kurtatchi**, as well as the **Lisu** of southern China, had "*lovemaking...as spontaneous on the part of one sex as of the other*". In some other cultures, such as the Polynesian **Maori** or the **Mataco** of South America, women generally initiated sexual encounters, while in many cultures women are discouraged from doing so.

A practice called *nikah ijtimah* ("combined marriage") existed in pre-Islamic **Arabia**, as reported in a Muslim hadith. A woman would arrange for a sexual tryst with "less than ten" men at one time. If she became pregnant, after she gave birth she would call for all her partners. Of her partners, she would name the one she preferred, and that partner would be considered the father of the child. He could not refuse this position. This was outlawed by Muslim law.

Many cultures practiced (or still practice) *polygyny*, which is the marriage of one man to multiple women. This was practiced in **India**, among **Muslims**, in **Myanmar**, in **China**, in **Tibet**, in **Egypt**, in **Kenya**, and so on. The opposite of polygyny is *polyandry*, where one woman would marry multiple men. This was also common in many regions and amongst many peoples, including the **Masaai** of Kenya, the Central Asian **Ye-Tai**, in **Bhutan**, around the Great Lakes of **Central Africa**, among the **Sherpa** people of Nepal, and so on. In many cases marriages of both types were done for practical purposes, such as keeping family inheritance together. However, several polygynous cultures had hostile reactions to the concept of polyandry, indicating (among other things) that there was a gender inequality component to be found as well.

The Abrahamic religions (Judaism, Christianity and Islam) were sexually defined by two major things: firstly, a Germanic-style disgust of sex outside of marriage, and secondly, a contempt for homosexuality and other "deviant" forms of behavior. For this reason, many cultures who adopted Abrahamic religions lost their old traditions and ways and came to accept these new values. Christianity, especially, glorified chastity as a virtue in its own right, often demonizing sexuality even within marriage as being tainted by original sin. In contrast to these, Hinduism states that the pursuit of sensual pleasures (*kama*) is as good and valuable alongside living morally (*dharma*) and self-actualization (*moksha*). Marital fidelity is still considered important, and the status of women is less than equal, but sexuality is not demonized in the same way.

Next, we come to the topic of age - although we briefly forayed into the issue when discussing pederastic homosexual relationships. Different cultures have radically different ideas about the proper age of adulthood and age of consent, and differences about that age provides a sticking point for cross-cultural interactions even today. Some cultures treated puberty as the defining point for consent, including the **Romans**, **Slavs**, **Indians** and most of medieval **Europe**. However, there are exceptions to this norm.

The **Germanic** peoples of the Iron Age were recorded as delaying sex until their twenties. The Roman historian Tacitus wrote that "*The youths partake late of the pleasures of love, and hence pass the age of puberty unexhausted: nor are the virgins hurried into marriage; the same maturity, the same full growth is required*". Pre-marital sex was strongly condemned, as was extra-marital sex, meaning that these late marriages were the only "acceptable" sexual activity for a Germanic individual.

While puberty was the point of the *legal* age of consent in medieval Europe, in effect this was only practiced by noble families (who arranged marriages for political purposes). Among commoners, marriages are recorded at older ages. In 14th and 15th century **England**, women and men married at between 18 and 22 years, and the age of the partners was similar. The average age rose in the 16th century - 25 for women, and 27 for men. Urban people are recorded as marrying slightly later than rural people. The English patterns were copied in the Low Countries (the **Netherlands** and **Belgium**) and Lowland **Scotland**. By the Elizabethan Era, medical journals stated that consummation before age 18 was harmful to both men and women. As a sidenote, Juliet's young age in *Romeo & Juliet* was intentionally designed to be an example of the harmful folly of youth, which makes it ironic that some people see it as simply being a norm of the times.

The final topic is that of <u>incest</u>. Direct incest between immediate family members ("nuclear incest" in modern parlance) was almost always condemned, regardless of the culture. Relationships between cousins, however, were more common - especially among royalty and nobility, who had strong reasons to keep ties between family lines.

The concept of *xwēdōdah*, originating in the *Zoroastrian* religion of **Iran**, is not only a toleration of nuclear incest but a ringing endorsement of it. According to the *Encyclopedia Iranica,* marriage between father and daughter, mother and son, or siblings was considered a pious action. It is described throughout early Iranian history; for example, the 3rd century priest Kartir describes roaming the country performing such marriages. Legal texts would describe the act as being beneficial for rulers and nobles, as it allowed inheritance to stay in the family, and allowed women to be controlled without being sent off to another patrilineal family group. However, it must be noted that the act had a religious and societal element that was just as strong - the act of incest itself was considered good, even if it produced no children.

Xwēdōdah has origins in the Zoroastrian creation myth, which states it was designed by Ahura Mazda (the religion's sole God) to "connect and guide" humans through their existence. In some models, Ahura Mazda mated with his mother to produce the sun and his sister to produce the moon. Other texts provide similar examples, but the core concept of Ahura Mazda designing, and partaking in, nuclear incest is a common thread. In many Zoroastrian texts, xwēdōdah is described as having a "cleansing" effect, being able to wash away certain sins. Perhaps ironically to modern eyes, one of the sins that *cannot* be washed away is anal intercourse, which is seen as a filthy and debauched act. It is worth noting that the homosexual pederastic practice of bacha bazi only showed up in Iran long after Zoroastrianism had become marginalized in importance.

Among the Pharaohs of **Egypt**, incest was relatively common, and marriages between immediate family - including polygamous marriages - were possible. This was done because the royal family of Egypt saw itself as divine in nature, and thus endogamous relationships were necessary to preserve their divinity. Like the Zoroastrian model, this belief was based on the actions of the Egyptian gods, and the mortal desire to carry on their model. When Egypt was taken over by the **Greek** *Ptolemaic* dynasty, the practice of incest was eventually continued, although for different, more practical reasons. Such cases show up in the twilight years of the dynasty's power, as the Ptolemaic family was trying to hold onto their land and power. In both cases, the prevalence of incest among the royal family did not indicate any level of incest among the common people.

A similar royal model existed among the **Inca**. Like the Egyptians, the Inca believed their royal family was divine in nature. In the later years of the Incan Empire, it was believed that only a pairing of a fully-blooded brother and sister could produce a true royal heir. In one case, a civil war erupted between two claimants: one the product of the previous king and his sister, and the other borne of a non-royal woman. The second claimant was Atahualpa, who would win the throne only to be confronted by the Spanish conquest of Francisco Pizarro. As such, he was the last Incan ruler.

2.5 Cultural Exchange

Once we have laid out a culture and the traits it consists of, the last logical step is connecting that culture to other cultures to form a greater world. This is what is called cultural exchange. Culture spreads by two main vectors. The first vector is <u>expansion</u>, being carried naturally as a culture expands and spreads. The descendants of a culture spread to different regions, carrying their traditions with them, but evolving in different ways. This is, for example, why there were **Celtic** nations across Europe, split into sub-groups such as the **Britons, Gauls**, and **Iberians**. Remember that cultural development has its roots in community; when communities are separated from each other, they grow in different ways. Expansion requires either a "blank slate", where immigrants inhabit an empty territory, or it requires the existing population to be driven out. This latter scenario was the case in ancient **Japan**; the indigenous **Emishi** and **Ainu** people were driven out and the victorious **Yamato** people took over their lands flat-out, spreading their own cultural values as they did.

The second vector is <u>assimilation</u>. This is when a culture convinces another culture to adopt its traditions, either through conquest and enforcement or more indirect influence. There are many examples of conquest-based assimilation. Empires such as the **Romans, Arabs** and **Chinese** each had their own process (*Romanization, Arabization*, and *Sinicization*, respectively). Their own values were prioritized; outsiders who adhered were rewarded, while outsiders who stayed true to their own traditions were punished. In 19th century **America**, native peoples were assimilated through policies and programs such as the Native Boarding Schools, designed to turn native children into "Americanized" adults.

Sometimes this could be reversed; Crusading **Franks** in the 12th century conquered parts of the Holy Land, establishing the so-called Crusader States. Their children, who retained Frankish tradition but were raised among Arabs, were called *Poulains*, meaning "foals". Poulains were noted by several contemporary writers (including James of Vitry and Fulcher of Charles) to have adopted many **Arabic** customs, such as regular bathing and local fashions, which earned them confusion or scorn from newly arrived European immigrants. The **Romans** made a regular habit of adopting useful ideas from conquered people, whether military, domestic, or artistic. In this way, conquest and invasion could be a two-way street of influential ideas. The **Mongols** conquered **China** under Genghis Khan, but under his descendant Kublai Khan the Mongols partially assimilated into Chinese culture, trading their nomadic ways for civilized luxuries.

Indirect influence, on the other hand, is dependent more on subtle exchange of ideas, such as frequent trading or intermarriage. **Sicily** in the 11th through 13th century is an example of many cultures mixing relatively peacefully; it was controlled by **Normans** (**French**-speaking **Norse** people), and populated with a mix of Orthodox **Greek** citizens and more recent Muslim **Arab** settlers. Somehow, despite all these cultures and three major religions, the Normans held it together with tolerant policies and thoughtful interactions. The resulting mix was known as the Norman-Arab-Byzantine Culture.

Cultural expansion creates "cousin cultures" - cultures that differ from their source culture, but still have things in common. Cultural assimilation creates cultures that have a set of original traits either influenced or overwhelmed by other cultures. So how do we discuss the finer mechanics?

Language is a good place to start. Language is the medium by which ideas are transmitted, and that includes values, rituals and beliefs. As a result, exchange between different regions and groups of people is easier when they have a common language. Language and communication also humanize people; a human being that cannot be communicated with was often perceived as an animal. The term "barbarian" originates from ancient **Greek**, where it was used to refer to anyone who did not speak Greek. It was based on the term "barbar", which, in several Indo-European languages, referred to stammering or unintelligible speech. Therefore, a "barbarian" was anyone whose speech was not understandable, and thus who could not be humanized.

Without linguistic connection or translation, cultural exchange is impossible.

Modern linguistics groups languages into families, which share common roots and therefore certain structures. For example, the *Romance* languages refers to Latin-derived languages such as **French**, **Spanish** and **Italian**. However, the Romance languages are only part of a larger linguistic family, the *Indo-European* family, which covers everything from Europe to **Russia** to **Iran** to **India**. The common ancestor of all these languages is "Proto-Indo-European", which dates back to the end of the Stone Age. Another major language family is the *Afro-Asiatic* family, which covers north Africa and the Arabian peninsula. Afro-Asiatic cultures include **Arabic**, **Hausa** and **Oromo**, among many others. There are many cultures across the islands of southeast Asia (**Indonesia** and the **Philippines**), but most of these cultures fall into the shared roots of the *Austronesian* family - as does the culture of **Madagascar**, which was partially colonized by far-reaching Polynesian immigrants.

If shared language represents a kind of unity, then differing languages are a barrier that must be overcome to create communication between cultures. In many cases, a *lingua franca*, or common language, is used across multiple regions to allow for intermediary communications. For example, in the medieval Mediterranean region, **Italian** was a common lingua franca spoken as a second language by many **Greeks**, **Arabs**, **Turks** and other regional peoples. This allowed these peoples to communicate with each other while maintaining their own linguistic traditions. Other examples of this include the **Sogdian** language in central Asia, **Malay** in southeast Asia, and **Hausa** in west Africa.

Developing a common language is also a key component of cultural assimilation. Within the **Roman** Empire, Latin (the language of the core territories) was used as a common official language in outer areas. These regions had populations who spoke their own language, but who also spoke Latin in order to communicate with their rulers. Other examples of this include *Nahuatl* in the **Aztec** Empire, *Amharic* in

Ethiopia, and languages such as **English**, **French** and **Spanish** in their far-flung colonies.

Religion is another element that can bind cultures together. Religious unity generally comes in two forms. The first form is when the dominant religion of a given culture can be shared with other cultures. In early history, this was accomplished through either conquest or immigration. Overarching regional religions would be carried by migrant peoples as they settled or invaded new regions, and those religious tenets would tie them to their ancestral home.

Widespread religious unity became increasingly common with the emergence of *Christianity*, *Islam* and *Buddhism*, which appealed to a wide range of people instead of being "region-specific". Such religions introduced the concept of *missionaries* - individuals who converted other cultures through relatively peaceful means without the need for total conquest and assimilation. There were also more earthly aspects to conversion: Christianity and Islam required obedience to a larger earthly authority, such as the Catholic Pope or the Caliphs of Islam. Islam in particular also required that believers make a pilgrimage to Mecca at least once in their lives.

In some cases, regions that became isolated would develop or maintain their own traditions; the Christian kingdoms of **Ethiopia** maintained Miaphysite beliefs even as the rest of the Christian world was divided between Catholic and Orthodox. In **Iran**, a group of Nestorian Christian communities formed the "Church of the East". Separated from both the Catholic and Orthodox churches, they pushed Christian beliefs into India, China and even Mongolia. Genghis Khan's grandson Mongke was a Nestorian Christian, following his mother's beliefs, and under his rule Nestorianism became the primary religion of the Empire. The activities of the Nestorian church led to legends being told in Europe about "Prester John", a king said to rule a far-off Christian empire.

In the second form, the local religion of an area can share common ancestors with other religions, creating recognizable patterns in their myths and legends. The Proto-Indo-European culture, mentioned earlier as a common language root, also served as a religious root for many cultures. Archetypes like "Sky Father" and "Goddess of Dawn" provide the roots for many pantheons - compare the **Indo-European** *Perkwunos* to the *Vedic Parjanya* or the **Lithuanian** *Perkunas*. When the **Greeks** and **Romans** encountered other peoples, they often characterized their deities in terms of their own religions, such as "the Scythian Ares". This is obviously looser than the first form, but it can create understandable parallels between cultural groups.

A <u>common enemy</u> is often necessary to bring together disparate groups with a shared culture. In many ways, cultural identity is identified as much by what you *aren't* as by what you *are*. The rise of nationalism in the 19th century was characterized most prominently by opposition to foreign rule. This was true of the European peoples subjugated by the **Ottomans** or the **Austro-Hungarian** Empire. It was also true of displaced **African** slaves forced to develop a new "Black" identity, and it was true of the many regions under **European** colonial control. Long before those, though, there were examples of cultures grouping together with "cousins" as the result of outside interference (and often dissolving again once the threat had passed).

The disparate city-states of ancient **Greece** had different governments and lived separately from each other, but they were united by language and tradition. This meant that when Greece was threatened by **Iran** during the *Greco-Persian Wars*, these Greek states clung together against the outsider. Once the threat had passed, the Greek states lost their sense of unity. In the later *Peloponnesian War*, which pitted an Athenian-led alliance against a Spartan-led alliance, the Spartan side even accepted assistance from Iran. In many ways, the Peloponnesian conflicts were even more gruesome and destructive than the Greco-Persian conflict was.

The **Gallic** people came together against the invasions of **Rome**, specifically under Julius Caesar. The Gauls came together under Vercingetorix, leader of the Arverni tribe. However, there were two factors that complicated the Gallic unity. Firstly, Vercingetorix's father

Celtillus had been executed previously for attempting to control all of Gaul. This distaste for unity fed into the second factor, which was internal strife that Caesar intentionally exploited in order to weaken the Gallic alliance. The Aedui, for example, were a Gallic people who had joined the alliance, but previously had a very pro-Roman stance. Once the war was over, the Aedui resumed their role as Roman allies.

Another enemy of Rome was the **Germanic** hero Arminius. Arminius was originally an auxiliary officer attached to a Roman unit, and during that time he learned their tactics and methods. He left Roman service to lead his people, the Cherusci, against the Romans. Marshaling the aid of five other tribes, he defeated the Romans soundly at the Battle of the Teutoburg Forest. However, their confederation represented only about 10% of the Germanic peoples, and once the Romans had been removed he found himself warring with other Germans as often as he did the Romans. Finally, he was assassinated by members of his own tribe - like Celtillus, the reason was that he allegedly sought too much power and dominion over his own people.

One notable thing about the numerous wars between **European** settlers and the many **Native American peoples** is that there are relatively few instances of a "united native front". Most wars, especially involving the USA, were engaged against one or two tribes at a time, with other native peoples joining either the natives or the whites as they saw fit. One of the exceptions was *Pontiac's War* in 1763, wherein around 3500 warriors from 14 tribes gathered together to attempt to drive out the British. The impetus was a weakening of **French** power in North America; before, the Europeans had to negotiate with native tribes to maintain their own careful balance of power. Tribes would ally with European powers on and off, maintaining a relatively mercenary relationship with the European powers.

After the French were effectively driven out, the British had less competition, and thus less reason to desire the cooperation of the native peoples. Because of this, they often stopped honoring treaties altogether. They also colonized land much more forcefully than the French, who were content merely to trade. For this reason, native peoples in the Great Lakes region rose up against the British in a combined attempt to drive them out. While the war ended in a truce, the Native peoples saw it as a minor victory because the British government was forced to acknowledge them officially, granting them legislative rights. But later native resistance would lack the unity of Pontiac's War; even the rare exception, like the *Yakima War* of 1855-88, had some native peoples allied with American forces.

World Cultures

III. RITUAL & SPIRITUALITY

Religion is the means by which human beings attempt to explain the things that they can't explain normally. It is how they explain where things came from, it is how they explain where things go, and it is how they give meaning or purpose to their lives. As a result, religion plays a large role in motivating and creating many aspects of cultural development.

Note, too, that religion affects almost every aspect of a culture in some way, from art to morality to identity. For this reason, this chapter is going to focus purely on the aspects that are "singularly" religious, such as mythology, cosmology and ritual.

3.1 Gods & Pantheons

At the head of most spiritual systems are *gods*, powerful beings who
affect the world as a whole. Humans (i.e. *mortals*) generally must
submit to these beings to receive their blessing and protection. Gods
also dictate proper behavior for their worshipers and provide them with
a structure by which to shape their lives.

<u>Monotheistic</u> religions tend to be built around the idea of a singular
God as an absolute creator, often infallible and all-knowing. This is
true of the *Abrahamic* religions (Judaism, Christianity and Islam)
originating in the Middle East, as well as the *Sikhism* of northern **India**.
The Sikh God, Ik Onkar, is described as formless (*nirankar*),
omnipresent (*sarav viāpak*) and beyond time and space (*akaal purkh*).
Ik Onkar cannot be known by physical senses, but can be connected to
by meditation and spiritual purification. In Abrahamic religions, God is
depicted as *all-knowing* in addition to other things; this is what grants
him the moral authority to determine what is right and wrong. In
Deuteronomy 29:19, it is stated that a person attempting to follow their
own moral compass rather than God's instructions will bring disaster
upon themselves. While such threats are common in other religions,
monotheism in particular prefers the idea of a lone, infallible deity who
is the source of all proper morality.

A slight alternative to monotheism is *henotheism*, which has one
supreme deity with characteristics similar to an absolute monotheistic
God, but underneath that supreme God are other gods, whether good or
evil in nature. **Iranian** *Zoroastrianism*, for example, is sometimes
described as henotheistic. There is a good and righteous creator (*Ahura
Mazda*) who is served by lesser deities (*yazatas*) in his fight against the
darkness of *Ahriman*. The difference between such a system and a
monotheistic system featuring divine servants such as angels can be
thin at times. However, in Zoroastrianism, the yazatas are worshiped in
the same way as gods in a polytheistic system. There is a branch of
Zoroastrianism called *Zurvanism* that says Ahura Mazda and Ahriman
are twin deities, and the actual "creator" deity is Zurvan, a morally
neutral being serving as the embodiment of time.

In the *Orthodox Christianity* of the **Byzantine Empire**, a schism within the church occurred when the veneration of saints (*douleia*) was considered to be a form of henotheism. The issue was whether or not the saints were being accorded worship that belonged only to God, and whether pictures of the saints constituted "graven images". This led to the Islam-inspired idea of *iconoclasm*, wherein icons and pictures depicting religious figures (including Jesus) were destroyed. However, this idea was eventually stamped out and declared heretical. After that, the church made a clear distinction between true worship of god (*latria*) and the veneration of saints, angels and relics. *Islam* also has a history of venerating saints, and had its own movement against this - the puritanical *Wahhabism* of the 18th century.

Another monothestic system is *monolatrism*, where a single god is worshipped, but the existence of other gods (i.e. gods of other cultures) is acknowledged. This is an inclusive form of worship often connected to the idea of "national gods", which were sometimes monotheist and sometimes the head of a polytheistic pantheon. An example of the latter is Tengri, who was their national god and the spiritual father of the **Turkish** peoples of central Asia. In the earliest records, the Abrahamic deity Yahweh was himself a monolatrist local god - the "national god" of Israel and Judah, in the same way that Qos was god of the **Edomites**, Ashur was the god of the **Assyrians**, or Zalmoxis was the god of the **Thracian Getae**. As time passed, Yahweh's importance was increased until he was part of an absolutist, exclusionary monotheism - a response to a similar development in Assyrian religion at the time. The transition between the two had the effect of increasing the power and legitimacy of the new monotheistic deity, while delegitimizing all others. Many foreign deities were cast as agents of Satan rather than "gods" in their own right. The **Caananite** deity Ba'al, for example, was established as the "Lord of Flies" Beelzebub.

Polytheism is the idea that there are many gods, forming a ruling *pantheon*. A core difference between monotheism and polytheism is that, by their nature, polytheistic deities are powerful, but imperfect. Polytheistic deities are arranged around specific spheres of influence, whether natural features (the sun, the oceans, thunder) or more abstract concepts (war, wisdom, leadership). Polytheistic deities are also fallible, with distinct personalities and flaws of their own.

In **Egyptian** mythology, the gods were depicted as being very human in nature, bearing the same fundamental needs and desires as mortals. The gods of **Norse** mythology were strong and long-lived, but not invulnerable - in fact, their own immortality was artificial, the result of the golden apples grown by the Goddess Iðunn. Norse mythology even comes with an identifiable endpoint - the climactic battle of *Ragnarok*, where the gods and their enemies destroy each other in one final fight. The **Gaelic** deity Nuada lost his arm in a battle, which disqualified him from leadership; he was allowed to retake his throne later when he received a prosthetic arm made of silver. These sorts of weaknesses are common in most polytheistic systems, which creates the necessity for multiple gods to fulfill multiple roles.

In polytheism, the gods are often a connected family composing a larger "divine race". This is true of the *Olympians* of **Greek** mythology, the *Aesir* and *Vanir* of **Norse** mythology, the *Kami* of **Japanese** mythology, the **Gaelic** *Tuatha De Dannan*, and the many gods of **Egyptian** mythology. These pantheons sometimes have outlying gods who do not belong to the family, but the family proper makes up the core set of divinities. Sometimes, their bloodlines extend to humanity. Greek gods such as Zeus were famous for coupling with mortals, creating half-divine offspring. In Egypt, the Pharaohs were believed to come from divine stock; this was also true of the Imperial family in Japan.

In many cases there are similar supernatural races that oppose the "divine race". The Gaelic gods fought both the *Fir Bolg* and the *Fomoire* for control of Ireland, the Greek gods fought their predecessors, the *Titânes*, the Norse gods fought the *Jötnar*, and the *Vedic* deities of **India** (or *Devas*) fought against the *Asuras*. Conflict is also a central component of Monotheistic religions, but there is a much more important moral element in monotheism, whereas polytheism may treat it in a more "neutral" way.

However, that is not always the case; in some religions, the gods are a powerful force protecting humanity from things that only they are capable of handling. In these cases, worship of the gods and sacrifices to them are justified as being necessary to empower the gods and support their fight against their enemies. In **Aztec** myth, the war god Huitzilopochtli fights non-stop against the *Tzitzimitl*, or "star goddesses". If he fails, then the world will be destroyed by earthquakes, as it had been destroyed several times before. It was the job of mortals to strengthen Huizilopochtli through sacrifice and war, as their failure would lead to *his* failure, and the fifth end of the world. The Aztecs developed many complex systems to ensure that there were enough human sacrifices to satisfy their religious requirements, including the *Flower Wars* that will be discussed in a later chapter. In **Egyptian** myth, the gods uphold *ma'at*, which is the concept of natural order, against *isfet*, chaos. Ma'at was necessary for the world to function normally - for the sun to rise and set, for tides to ebb and flow, and so on. Mortals could also aid ma'at by living virtuously, or harm it by living villainously. They could also aid the gods in their fight against isfet through prayer, the offering of sacrifices, or the conducting of rituals.

In others, the relationship between gods and mortals was more mercenary. In **Sumerian** mythology, the relationship between gods and humans is made more clear, in a way that may have applied to many other polytheistic religions. In the *Epic of Gilgamesh*, the gods destroy humanity with a flood. The only humans to survive are Utnapishtim, his family, and craftsmen from his village. Utnapishtim builds an ark and loads it with grain and animals. When the flood waters recede, Utnapishtim makes a sacrificial offering of animals, which the gods gather greedily around. Through this, it is known that the gods did not consider their own need for sacrifice and worship, and they admit their fault in aiding the destruction of their own livelihoods. In the **Greek** religion, the Olympians were not even involved with the creation of humanity, nor do they serve as its primary patrons. Both of those roles were taken up by the Titan Prometheus, who was punished by Zeus for his trouble. Throughout his existence, Zeus often took an antagonistic role with humans, punishing them for hubris or as a potential threat. The human relationship with the divine was thus more explicable as the capricious favors and disfavors of powerful beings, rather than the inexplicable anger and rage of a supposedly benevolent father.

Another common trait of polytheism is the ability to adapt new gods into their pantheon. In ancient **Rome**, the core pantheon is sometimes said to have been taken from the Greek Olympians, but this may have been a later development, an evolution of native Roman deities based on their emulation of Hellenic culture. What is known is that foreign deities such as the **Iranian** god Mithras were often welcomed into the traditional Roman religion. Sometimes religions were fused, such as the *Gallo-Roman* religion, wherein the gods of the conquered **Gallic** peoples were combined with **Roman** gods based on their sphere of influence. One Gallic deity - Epona, Goddess of Horses - was brought into the Roman religion entirely. The methods of worship were also frequently combined. Certain religions, such as the aforementioned Mithras, were "mystery religions", whose tenets and participation were limited to those who had passed certain tests. When *Christianity* overtook the empire, these religions were persecuted particularly hard due to suspicion of their nature. Similar integration was found in **Chinese** polytheism. While there is a large core group of Chinese deities, such as Yudi, the Jade King, Doumu, the Queen of Heaven, and Shennong, patron of peasants and farmers, there are also gods taken from neighboring areas such as **India** and **Mongolia**. For example, Xiàngtóushén (Elephant-Headed God) is the *Hindu* deity Ganesh in a different form. Furthermore, there are many regional differences between different parts of China, as well as philosophical and spiritual interpretations of shared core concepts.

The *Dharmic* religions of **India** deserve some special attention due to their complexity. One of the earliest forms of Indian religion was the *Vedic* religion. This was a polytheistic pantheon derived from the same Indo-Aryan roots that would later form into the Greek and Norse religions. The gods of Vedism were the benevolent *Devas*, who fought against the malign *Asuras*. However, around 500 BCE, the Vedic religion began to split with the ascendance of new schools of thought: the *Hindu, Buddhist,* and *Jain* religions. Buddhism and Jain were more spiritual in nature, being centered around enlightenment rather than worship - although Buddhism still kept aspects of polytheism. Hinduism, on the other hand, merged many of the old Vedic deities with a new core of multi-faceted henotheism. Hinduism introduced three deities who each represented aspects of a supreme God. These were *Brahma*, representing creation, *Vishnu*, representing preservation, and *Shiva*, representing destruction. Compared to the earlier Vedic Devas, these newer Gods were more cosmic in scale, symbolizing the beginnings and ends of life and existence itself.

Hinduism has no central authority and thus it is practiced in many different ways and following many traditions. Some schools of Hinduism focus on the monolatrist worship of a single deity, such as *Shaivism* for Shiva, *Vaishnavism* for the god Vishnu, or *Shaktism* for the goddess Shakti. Even within these specific belief systems there are further differences based on interpretations of the god and their roles. It is therefore easiest to say that Hinduism encompasses many different belief systems and styles of worship, bound together by a shared mythology and general belief system.

3.2 Spirits & Souls

The previous chapter discussed the ruling entities of spiritual systems. However, there are many other aspects of religious belief that exist and that shape the way that the world is perceived by worshipers. Most of these concepts exist in conjunction with monotheism or polytheism, although certain cultures have no true "gods" and only believe in spiritual elements.

Animism is the idea that all things possess a spirit or soul. This includes living things (animals, plants), non-living items (stones, man-made objects), and more abstract concepts such as rivers, mountains and celestial entities. In practice, animism involves treating all things as at least partially sacred. For example, if an animal is killed, its body must be treated respectfully, and the proper rituals must be conducted to allow its spirit to pass on.

Animist concepts can be found in many polytheistic or even monotheistic religions. In some cases, the difference between a powerful spirit and a god comes down to nothing more than whether or not the being is worshiped. The *Shinto* religion of **Japan** has many animist beliefs alongside its core polytheistic pantheon. *Ko-Shinto*, the native belief system of the **Emishi** and **Ainu** peoples, has less of a divide between its animistic elements and its polytheistic elements, since the spirits that are worshiped are their "gods". The religion of the **Sami** people of northern Scandinavia is also polytheistic with animist elements.

However, in some cases, animism exists without worship, which is to say that the people who hold that belief hold no sense of obligation or subservience to the spirits. The *Bori* religion of the west African **Hausa** people was based on a world of spirits, or *iskoski*. These spirits could be communicated with and appealed to with the proper rites. Many were associated with a particular region or landmark (for example, a tree) and sacrifices could be left for them there. Iskoski were capable of possessing individuals, and could then speak through their mouths to offer advice or warnings. Many Iskoski were identified with specific names and titles, but unlike a polytheistic system they were not "gods".

In the religion of the **Anishinaabe** peoples of the American Great Lakes region, the world is filled with spiritual beings called *manidoog*. Manidoog could be positive or negative in nature, and reflected both natural forces and monsters such as the *wendigo*. In some traditions there is also a *Giche Manidoo*, or great spirit, that fulfills a gentle monotheistic role. Because the Anishinaabe traditions are carried by oral tradition, some sources are unclear, and some historians believe that the Giche Manidoo was developed as a response to Christian influences.

Two other concepts fall under the general animist umbrella. *Shamanism* ties into the concept of an animist "spirit world", and refers to the practice of using meditation, fasting, or drugs to connect to that spirit world. This is used for several purposes - communing with ancestors, seeking information from spirits, or solving problems such as sickness or infertility. Shamans traditionally play an important role in their societies, serving as mediators and counsel for the community as a whole. Examples of shamanistic societies can be found throughout the world, from Asia to Europe to Africa to North America.

Totemism is the belief in tutelaries - spirits that serve as the patrons and guardians of families, places, or individuals. Totemism comes in many different forms. The word "Totem" comes from the **Ojibwe** people, who marked their clans with totemic animals. One's lineage would be marked by the totems of one's father or mother, and marriage had to be arranged with someone of a different totem. This system is also used by aboriginal **Australians**, the **Nor** of Papau New Guinea, the **Birhor** and **Marathi** of India, and others. Another type of totem was a protective icon used to mark or defend a given region. For example, the *jangseung* of **Korea** were poles with carved faces posted around the edge of a village both as territory markers and to keep away evil spirits. In **Thailand**, pillars called *lak mueang* are commonly found inside cities, and serve as a house for the city's protective spirit.

The <u>afterlife</u> is where the mortal spirit goes after death. Almost every religion describes such a place, and its existence plays a central role in the purpose of faith. Depending on the afterlife and its rules, there can be huge ramifications for the behavior of the living, because the promise or threat of a given afterlife sets a goal for human life.

The afterlife of **Mesopotamian** religions was described in different ways by different myths and accounts. In some, the underworld was described as a dismal, gray place. The spirits of the dead dwelled in darkness and had nothing to eat except clay and dust. For this reason, funerary offerings were very important, as they provided the only comforts for the dead. One story, *"The Death of Ur-Namma"*, describes the passage of a king after death. The titular king, Ur-Namma, made use of the offerings he was buried with to please the other inhabitants of the underworld and the gods, which earned him a position of authority in the underworld's bureaucracy. It is indicated during the story that other mortals have taken the same route as him. The idea of providing goods or luxuries for the deceased could also be found in other cultures, including **Egyptian**, **Norse**, **Chinese**, and **Etruscan** societies. In some cases, slaves or servants would be sacrificed in order to continue serving their owner in the afterlife. In **Greek** culture, a dead body had coins placed over its eyes, which would be used to pay the ferryman, Charon, for passage into the next world.

Many societies practice ancestor-veneration, which is founded in the belief that the deceased continue to influence the world and give good or bad luck to their descendants. To that end, ancestors are honored with shrines, periodic offerings, and virtuous behavior. This is true in most Asian countries, including **China**, **Korea**, **Japan**, **Thailand**, **Vietnam**, **Burma**, **The Philippines**, and **India**. In *Zhou*-period **China**, a ritual called a *shi* ceremony would allow an ancestor to enter a living person (the titular shi). The ancestor would eat and drink offered food and drink through their living body, converse with their modern descendants, and answer their questions.

In some religions, virtue is rewarded with a peaceful and benevolent afterlife, while misdeeds are punished by eternal torture. In the **Greek** afterlife, the soul exits the body after death and goes to the banks of the river Styx. If the deceased individual's relatives have supplied them with the proper fare (a coin placed under the tongue) they are ferried across to the judges of the underworld. These judges determine where the soul will spend eternity. Heroes and the especially virtuous would go to Elysium, where they dwelled in ease. Average people would go to the Fields of Asphodel, which is described as a foggy place, where spirits of the dead dwell restlessly, without thought or identity. The particularly wicked would be sentenced to eternal torture in the Fields of Punishment; many of these individuals had custom-made labors meant to fit their crime.

One alternative to traditional afterlife (i.e. "the spirit goes to the underworld and stays there") is the concept of reincarnation. Reincarnation is the idea that the spirit leaves the body and re-enters a new vessel in our material world. This is most distinctly part of the *Dharmic* religions of **India** - *Hinduism, Buddhism, Jainism* and *Sikhism*. However, it could also be found among certain branches of the **Celts, Greeks, Romans, Chinese** taoism, and Christianity. Different religions had different views on reincarnation and its purpose. In Hinduism, one's virtue would affect where one went after death - whether to the celestial realm, to earth, or to the infernal realm However, going to the celestial or infernal realm was not permanent, and bodies in those places could die just as a body on earth, providing another chance at reincarnation. In some cases, the afterlife was conflated with the dwelling of the gods. The **Celtic** and **Gaelic** afterlife was based within the "*Otherworld*". This was in many ways it was an alternate dimension that sometimes intersected with the "mortal" realm. However, certain heroic figures were able to find it by entering the "Western Sea". Souls of the dead would go to the Otherworld and stay there for a time until they were ready to reincarnate.

A feature of Dharmic reincarnation was the idea of achieving perfection or freedom. This is called by several different names, with the most common being *moksha* (for Hindus) or *nirvana* (for Buddhists). Essentially, the cycle of reincarnation (*samsara*) would continue until the individual had achieved the clarity necessary to

51

understand the universe and maintain virtue. This is seen as the ultimate goal of the Dharmic religions, comparable to the pursuit of Heaven in Abrahamic religions.

In certain parts of **Tibetan**, **Mongolian** and **Nepalese** culture (among others), the nature of reincarnation leads to the idea that a dead body is merely an empty shell, with the spirit having departed it. In order to dispose of the body "generously", the dead are left out to be eaten by carrion birds. This is called a "sky burial". In the *Zoroastrian* religion of **Iran**, a similar ritual is done; the deceased are placed on a stone step-pyramid called a *Tower of Silence* and left for the birds. Unlike its eastern counterpart, Zoroastrian sky-burials are conducted in order to avoid uncleanliness and disease, allowing the vultures to do the grisly work of disposing of the body.

Divination is the practice of telling the future or gaining information through ritual. These rituals were designed to communicate with gods, spirits or souls, who would provide answers by influencing the medium used. The modern *Ouija* board is a form of divination, for example. Divination was taken seriously as a form of divine or spiritual communication by most of the societies that practiced it.

Theriomancy was based on observing patterns of animal behavior, such as the *augury* of ancient **Rome**, **Greece** and **Germany** (using birds), the *myrmomancy* of Central Africa's **Zande** people (using ants) or the *nggàm* of Cameroon's **Mambila** people (using crabs).

Scrying was the act of gazing into a reflective item such as a mirror, crystal ball, or bowl of water to try to see something in it. Scrying is noted amongst the **Egyptians**, **Romans**, **Greeks**, **Iranians**, **Mayans**, and **Germanic** peoples.

Cleromancy was divination through luck, by casting dice or bones in such a way that spiritual intervention could reveal results. In **China**, this forms the basis of the "*Yi Jing*" (or "I Ching") method, which uses dice, yarrow stalks or coins to generate a binary set of hexagrams. Another Chinese method was *qiúqiān*, which involves the questioner taking a numbered stick out of a large group. The number translates to a result given by an interpreter. This was similar to the *sortes* of ancient **Rome**. According to the historian Tacitus, the **Germanic** peoples engaged in lot-based divination; a branch would be cut from a tree, then cut further into parts which would be marked. The parts would be thrown onto a white cloth and the result would be interpreted. Casting lots was also common in **Jewish** tradition as a method of communicating with God - allowing the divine to determine the results, rather than relying on sheer "luck" as in gambling.

Sometimes, divination would be done using parts of animals. *Hepatomancy* involved reading the liver of a sacrificed animal, and was practiced in the **Babylonians, Hittites, Etruscans** and **Romans**. The Roman practice (*haruspicina*) was taken from the Etruscans, who the Romans conquered early on in their history. One of the oldest **Chinese** models was the *oracle bone*, wherein a question would be carved onto a turtle shell, and then heat would be applied until the shell cracked. The cracks would determine the answer to the question. A similar practice was the **Japanese** method of *futomani*, which involved doing the same thing with a stag's shoulder-blade.

Using cards to tell fortunes is called *cartomancy*. Cartomancy in general showed up later in history than most other examples, because for "cards" to exist, there needs to be a way to produce them (i.e. paper and ink). The oldest cards date back to 10th century **China**, and made its way into **Persia** and **Egypt**. However, these cards were used solely for games. Cards came to **Europe** in the late 1300s, but were not used for divination until at least two centuries later, and were not used *regularly* for this purpose for another two. *Tarot* decks were originally used for games, but later became the primary medium for cartomancy. The idea of Tarot carrying occult significance originated in **France** as a result of its assumed Egyptian origins, which became linked to classical mythology and wisdom.

World Cultures

IV. SOCIAL STRUCTURE

The most basic elements of human society are centered around the family. However, when society gets larger, "family ties" often won't cut it. A large culture requires interaction and cooperation between lots of people who lack family ties; instead, those people are held together by common values and ideals, as well as the authority of a central figure or council.

4.1 Law & Government

A government is a group of people able to project power over a region, generally with the compliance (if not support) of the other people in that region. A government's power can be vested in a single person or it can be delegated amongst members of a community. A government is funded by taxing its constituents or subjects, either directly through tax collectors (such as the famed courier system of **Iran** during the *Achaemenid* dynasty) or by levying periodic tribute from vassal states. The *Islamic* Caliphates cared for their Muslim citizens by levying higher taxes, or *jizya*, on non-Muslims living in their territories.

The extent of a government's power, or its <u>borders,</u> are often more difficult to define than a modern audience might think. Firstly, borders are usually vague, even when the border is between two states who can come to an agreement about it. Obstructive landscape features such as rivers, mountains or man-made walls serve as relatively understandable borders. However, in open terrain, setting a true "border" is relatively difficult unless both parties have agreed on exact placement. In most cases, a government would designate border regions, or *marches*, instead of solid borders. A march would be patrolled by soldiers and watchmen, and the governor or noble in charge of a march (a *marquis*) would have additional military responsibilities and powers suitable to their role. The inhabitants of a march became used to the idea of having multiple "rulers", or perhaps no ruler at all.

Borders became more solid as the result of lawful ownership of land increasing in prominence. One look at a complicated state like the **Holy Roman Empire** shows that individual landowners or lords had their hands full determining where exactly they had ownership rights. In this way, solid borders are dependent on the cooperation of the parties involved, and there are usually legal ways to contest over territory.

Governments legitimize themselves by offering <u>services</u> to their constituents, such as protecting them from foreign invaders, dealing with domestic criminals, or ensuring economic stability. A well-developed government will include departments to handle those matters in addition to the staff necessary to maintain its own power. In Imperial **Rome**, the *vigiles urbani* ("watchmen of the city") served as both policemen and firefighters. They were paid for by the Emperor, and replaced a privately-driven market for those services which had proven inefficient at best and overtly corrupt at worst. Outside of the capital, the Roman legions served as law enforcement for the areas they were stationed in, protecting from both internal and external threats. Other cultures had institutions similar to the vigiles, such as the **Chinese** prefect system, the **Egyptian** *Medjay*, or the **French** and **Norman** constabulary. Less formalized cultures might simply see the law enforced by the community at large, or by the retinue soldiers of a local lord.

Any given culture has its own set of laws and values. In order to support those laws, punishments or penalties must be used against lawbreakers. This implied threat is one of the foundations of society, because it normalizes behavior and allows people to have a degree of trust in the group as a whole. The more confidence that people have in the reliability and fairness of law and order, the more orderly the society will be. Codified legal systems can be found all over the world from the very beginnings of civilization. The oldest of these is the Code of Ur-Nammu, a 22nd century BCE **Sumerian** system recorded on tablets. The Code consisted of "if-then" statements centered around punishment or compensation.

There are essentially two major types of legal case. The first of these is "civil law". Civil law is centered around injustices or imbalances between private parties (i.e. individuals or families, rather than governments). For example, in many societies, if one party injures or harms another, they will pay restitution or compensation to that party. In short, the payment is meant to make up for the damage done, and the legal system exists to act as a threat to ensure the payment is carried out. Many cases in civil law were relatively low-level, dealing with theft or financial damages, and these were often handled with fines paid to the victim. But serious charges, most notably murder, could also be handled within the confines of civil law.

The most "polite" manner of handling murder was called *blood money*. It was essentially an extension of the compensatory model: financial restitution for a killing, paid by the killer to the victim's family. In **Islam**, this was called *diyya*, and applied when a Muslim killed another Muslim. It is also a part of the **Somali** legal system, or *xeer*. Amongst the **Germanic**, **Norse** and **Frankish** peoples, it was called *wergild* (or "man-money"). In **Irish**, it was *eraic*; in **Welsh**, it was *galanas*, and in **Poland** it was called *głowszczyzna*. Each human life was given a price, with the cost dependent on the person's status and gender. Once payment was received, the matter would be considered settled. If there was no payment, it would usually lead to retributive violence. Not all sorts of killing were considered worthy of blood money; for the Germanic peoples, killing someone on holy ground, or while they slept, was worthy of criminal penalties regardless of payment. This was because it was a manner of public safety and decency, rather than a "normal" affair between two families.

A more violent alternative was the *blood law* practiced by some **Native American** peoples, such as the **Cherokee**. Blood law meant that if an individual was killed, his killer had to be killed by a close family member. In some cases the act was done by the killer's own tribe in order to appease the victim's family. It was about restoring balance and preventing inequality, which itself prevented blood feuds from developing. Revenge could not be pursued on a priest's property or on designated "towns of refuge". These rules were often used to force a trial, which was otherwise unnecessary. In contrast to feuds, blood law apparently did not result in retaliatory killings.

Pacifist cultures took these same impulses and tried to settle them in less destructive ways. Among the **Moriori** people of Polynesia, it was stated that "*...because men get angry and during such anger feel the will to strike, that so they may, but only with a rod the thickness of a thumb, and one stretch of the arms length, and thrash away, but that on an abrasion of the hide, or first sign of blood, all should consider honour satisfied.*" This quote comes from oral tradition, as told in "Moriori: A People Rediscovered" by Michael King. In essence, the

Moriori recognized that anger is a natural emotion, and combined with ego it can escalate into serious violence. But for both practical and ideological reasons, the Moriori found alternate ways to deal with these feelings that would mollify all parties.

However, if none of these practices satisfied the two parties, then a *feud* would occur. A feud is a situation in which both parties (whether families, clans or tribes) are engaged in a series of retaliatory killings, with each new killing creating justification for the next retaliation. In many cases, vengeance was ordained by religious right. A huge number of societies have included feuds as part of their cultural makeup, including all those mentioned in the entry for blood money. Feuds can be found in almost all regions of the globe, from Western Europe (**Celts, Gaels, Germans, Norse**) to the Mediterranean (**Greeks, Corsicans, Sardinians, Cretans, Cypriots, Arabs, Jews**) to Eastern Europe (**Serbs, Albanians, Kosovars, Chechens**) to West Asia (**Kurds, Pashtuns, Indians, Sikhs**) to East Asia (**Chinese, Filipino, Burmese, Japanese**) to Africa (**Somali, Ethiopian, Berbers**) to America (**Haudosaunee**). In many of these regions, feuding exists even today.

Feuding is often seen as a sign of a weak legal system that forces families to take punishment into their own hands. However, this was not always the case. Feuds were accepted as a legitimate legal outcome in many societies, although as a society advanced it tended to see them as a nuisance or public disorder. In 1495, the **Holy Roman Emperor** Maximilian I issued the *Ewiger Landfriede* (Eternal Peace), which outlawed feuding between noble families. The impetus was that the discord between nobility made it harder for imperial princes and emperors to manage these families. In 1873, the **Japanese** government outlawed *kataki-uchi*, their society's blood revenge system, for similar reasons. Prior to this, there are examples of kataki-uchi killings being legally accepted as justified (i.e. "not murder"), to the point that 15th century official Nakahara Yasutomi claimed that many murderers would try to establish their cases as kataki-uchi in order to get away with the crime.

The other major type of law is <u>criminal law</u>, wherein the government deals with lawbreakers directly. This is a form of punishment based not on the damages done to the victim, but the fact that the criminal transgressed society's laws. Many cases have both a civil and a criminal element; for example, murder can be both a civil issue (reparations to victim's family) and a criminal issue (breaking a law against murder). In some regions and time periods, civil arrangements were effectively the only laws, whereas the existence of a criminal law system implies a strong, authoritative governmental entity with the authority and power to carry out such punishments.

Use of the death penalty was common in many ancient societies. In many early legal systems, such as the Code of Ur-Nammu or the **Hittite** Code of the Nesilim, death was essentially the only "criminal" penalty, with all other issues being handled by civil law payments to the victim. However, as societies developed, more nuanced punishments became desirable or feasible.

The concept of exile was one alternative to capital punishment. In essence, the individual would be removed from the area (city, province or nation) and not allowed to return. The laws of Draco, in ancient **Athens**, dictated that exile was the punishment for murder, although this could be mediated if the killer apologized and the family of the victim accepted the apology. Relatedly, Draco's law system made it illegal for a member of the victim's family to kill a suspect, though they were allowed to hunt down the suspect and bring him to the authorities. When Draco's unpopular legal system was overturned and replaced by the laws of Solon, the laws concerning murder were kept relatively intact. Banishment was also used by the **Roman** government, introduced as a measure to avoid the over-usage of the death penalty. The poet Ovid was sent into exile by Emperor Augustus because of what he called *carmen et error*, "a poem and a mistake". Further details were the cause of intense speculation both at the time and by modern historians.

Another Athenian practice called *ostracism* allowed for the exile of a citizen by vote. At a yearly assembly, the citizens were asked if they would like an ostracism performed. If they voted yes, another vote would be held two months later. This vote was open-ended; the citizens would give the name of a citizen they desired to be ostracized to a scribe, who would then write it on a shard of pottery (paper being too expensive to use for such disposable notes). The citizen with the most votes for ostracism (some sources say at least 6,000 were required) would be banished from the city for ten years. A notable feature of this process is that there was no trial or defense; the democratic assembly was asked if it wanted to remove someone, and if it did, it did. However, the targets of ostracism were usually agreed-upon enemies of the state or potential tyrants, and in any case the penalty of exile was not as harsh as many penalties the Athenian courts were able to carry out. After the Athenian form was developed, other **Greek** city-states picked up the pattern, including **Syracuse**, which used olive leaves instead of pottery.

A more severe form of exile was *outlawry*, sometimes called *civil death*, which strips the protection of law from the individual. In many cases, outlawing someone was the most severe form of punishment, because anything could be done to them without legal repercussion. Among the **Germanic** and **Norse** peoples, outlawry was the ultimate penalty, used to punish rape, incest, adultery and treason. Notably, most aspects of early Germanic law were based on compensation (i.e. fines or wergild), and outlawry was the rare divergence from this system. Outlawry was used for crimes considered so heinous that people simply would not accept living with someone who had committed it. In some cases, outlawry would be followed by immediate killing, whereas in others the condemned individual would be allowed to escape into the wild.

In Rome, an outlaw was referred to as *homo sacer*, which meant both "the sacred man" and "the accused man". An individual declared *homo sacer* was a non-person who could be killed at will, but could not be sacrificed to the Gods. According to the *Duodecim Tabulae*, a legal document from 450 BCE, the punishment was often given to oath-breakers, since their crime was religious in nature. Another form of Roman outlawry, in the later Roman republic, was *interdicere aqua et igni*, or "interdiction of fire and water". In this system, a Roman citizen would be exiled. During this exile, they would retain their rights as a citizen. However, if they returned without permission, they would be outlawed. Any citizen who provided them with either fire or water would share their punishment - hence the name. Both of these punishments became very rare with the development of the Empire and a stronger foundation of criminal justice.

A related concept, also used by the Romans, was *proscription*. Unlike outlawry, proscription was usually more political in nature than judicial. In essence, proscription is the identification of an "enemy of the state". In Rome, it was used after certain individuals (such as Lucius Sulla) took power, and was applied en masse to their political enemies. A proscripted individual was essentially outlawed - but in addition, when he died his estate would be taken by the state (with some of it used as reward money for informants). Similar purges have existed throughout history; many were done wholly by the government or by a political faction, without the involvement of the common people.

An alternative to exile and outlawry was imprisonment. This was comparatively rare because an imprisoned individual consumed resources, and justice systems of the era were not particularly concerned with long-term rehabilitation. Early prisons, such as those in Greece or Rome, were used primarily to hold prisoners awaiting trial, rather than being long-term solutions on their own. Proper "prisons" did not become common in **Europe** until medieval times. This was based on a practice of Christian clergy called *detrusio*, which was used internally to punish wayward monks or priests in a manner that avoided bloodshed. By the 1300s, prisons had become a well-regulated feature in many cities, being managed by a consistent legal system. One specific type of prison was the *oubliette* (**French** for *forgotten*), where prisoners would be placed and then, as the name suggests, simply forgotten about until they starved to death.

Punishment by enslavement was slightly more common, because it provided benefits out of the accused. The Achaemenid Empire of **Iran**, which outlawed most types of slavery, allowed for the enslavement of prisoners-of-war and rebels because of the conditions of their capture. Even so, such slaves were meant to be treated well. This was not the case in Rome, where lower-class citizens who committed high crimes were legally enslaved and sentenced to hard labor. One particular type of slave labor was the *ergastulum*, a pit where slaves would be chained together in cramped, miserable conditions to do various types of work. Among the **Aztecs**, slavery was a possible punishment for certain crimes, such as murder, but also for those in debt or otherwise financially imperiled. In medieval times, the use of slaves as rowers became common, especially among Mediterranean powers like **France**, the **Italian** states, and the **Ottoman Empire**. Before then, galley rowers were respected freemen, with slaves being used in desperate situations (and in some cases, the slaves who did so were freed after they had served). Other forms of forced penal labor were common around the world, and many persist even in first-world countries to this day.

4.2 Caste & Class

Some societies have relatively fluid ideas about what people should do; while there may be a core separation between upper and lower classes, or freemen and slaves, that's as far as it goes. However, in some cultures, societal stratification is more in-depth and detailed than that. A caste system seeks to put people into categories that can be either descriptive or prescriptive. In the latter case, castes are generally enforced hereditarily, with marriages being arranged endogamously (i.e. between two members of the same caste). Caste systems are sometimes used to control commoners by increasing the effect that societal authority has on their comings and goings. For example, preventing farmers from becoming merchants, or keeping military power in the hands of the nobility.

The idea of an *untouchable* caste exists across many societies, from **India** (*dalit*) to **Japan** (*burakumin*) to **Tibet** *(ragyabpa)* to **Korea** (*baekjeong*) to the **Pyrenees** region (*Cagot*) to **Hawaii** (*kauwa*). Untouchables were a hereditary caste considered to be "outside" of normal society, who were used to do work considered unclean by others such as butchery or tanning. In Asia, their condition was generally associated with spiritual pollution and uncleanliness. The Cagots of southern France were distinct because the reason for their separation was not known, or at least not agreed upon, and despite this they were persecuted. Untouchables lived outside of "proper" towns in their own shanty districts. They were denied many of the rights of normal people, and were not allowed to intermarry with non-untouchables. In many cases they were denied spiritual rights, literacy, and any form of societal advancement.

In **India**, the *varna* separates people into four classes: *brahmin* (priests), *kshatriya* (warriors & rulers), *vaishya* (craftsmen, farmers and traders), and *shudra* (laborers). Outside them were the *dalit*, or untouchables. This is a descriptive system with religious importance; a member of a class was ideally meant to fulfill their societal role to the fullest. However, these classes were not necessarily hereditary in nature. That came when the varna was partially combined with *jāti*, a more complex family system that created thousands of endogamous groups across India. Members of different jāti do not marry, share food, or (if possible) make contact with each other at all. These castes had some overlaps, but they were not fully the same. For example, in **Sri Lanka**, the *Salagama* jāti were soldiers and cinnamon farmers - fitting the role of both kshatriya and vaishya in the varna model. The island of **Bali** uses a model based on the varna alone, without the complicating factors of the jāti.

Tibet built its government around the priesthood (the *lamas*, headed by the *Dalai Lama*). There were nine castes total, divided into three divisions: high, medium, and low. The high division was composed of the Dalai Lama himself at the top, the nobility (often family of a Dalai Lama or ancient royal family) below them, and high-ranking priests and monks below them. The middle division consisted of "taxpayer families" (large landowning family units), "householders" (individual landowners, with smaller land owned), and "lease peasants", who had to rent land. Finally, the low division consisted of untouchables, hereditary household servants, and slaves.

In **China**, the "four occupations" (*shi-nong-gong-shang*) were used to divide society. The *shi* were rulers, scholars and administrators, the *nong* were farmers, the *gong* were artisans, and the *shang* were merchants. Each role had certain privileges and values associated with it. The merchants were considered the "lowest" class, due to their inability to "produce", but many merchants became rich nonetheless. In the *Tang* dynasty (618-907 AD), and even moreso in the *Song* dynasty (960-1279), an individual could work up to the *shi* class by taking exams. This was meant to secure proper meritocratic placement within society. It should be noted that there were many jobs excluded from the four occupations system, such as soldiers, priests, and laborers. Soldiers, at least, were an intentional exclusion - the system of *wen* and *wu* emphasized respect for civility and distaste for violence. As such, soldiers were regarded as a necessary evil, not a glorified profession.

Japan had several caste periods based on their current government. In the 7th century, the Japanese court imitated the castes of the contemporary Tang dynasty. This was called *Ryosensei*, a combination of four upper-class castes (*ryōmin*) and five lower-class castes (*senmin*). The upper-class castes were *kanjin* (government officer), *kōmin* (citizen), *shinabe* (high merchant), and *zakko* (miscellaneous households). The lower-class castes were *ryōko* (imperial servants), *kanko* (public ministries), *kenin* (servants of noble families), *kunuhi* (court slaves), and *shinuhi* (slaves of other families).

In the later *Edo* period (1603-1868), under the *Tokugawa* shogunate, society was once again stratified. It was built on the four-occupations model used in China and was a formalization of an ongoing, but previously more casual, caste arrangement. Its solidification existed to prevent social mobility; for example, peasants often found it difficult to leave their villages in earlier periods, but it was theoretically possible. Under the new system, it was illegal for a peasant to abandon their fields, either to become a merchant or a "wage laborer". This was originally done as a wartime measure (for the invasion of Korea by Hideyoshi Toyotomi), but was kept in place for social reasons.

Under the *Joseon* dynasty (1392-1897), **Korea** possessed several castes: the *yangban* (aristocracy & military officers), the *chungin* (bureaucrats & administrative workers), the *sangmin* ("clean" commoners, such as farmers, merchants and craftsmen) and the *cheonmin* ("vulgar" commoners, such as butchers, metalworkers, magicians, and performers). Technically below the cheonmin were the "*nobi*", who were cheonmin taken legally by the yangban as slaves.

Iran under the *Sasanian* dynasty had a caste system with limited complexity at its core, but more in its execution. The 10th/11th century Iranian historian Al-Biruni described them as having four core castes: *Arteshtaran,* knights and princes, *Asravan,* monks, priests and lawyers, *Dabiran,* physicians and astronomers, and *Vasteryoshan,* husbandmen and artisans. Other sources describe the castes slightly differently (dabiran are secretaries, vasteryoshan are commoners in general). Most agree that the system had far more complexities based on region and ethnicity that the four-caste model did not cover.

In west Africa, there are several examples of caste-based societies. The **Mandé** empires of West Africa, including the empires of **Ghana**, **Mali** and **Songhai**, were built around "clan-based castes". In essence, one's clan determines one's profession, with the most common clan-castes being metalworkers, carpenters and fishermen. The **Soninke** people divided society into nobles (*Hooro*), "dependents" (*naxamala*), and slaves (*komo*), with distinct subdivisions among each group. Among the dependents, or common people, smiths held the most respect, because shaping metal had an almost magical mystique about it. Marriage outside caste was prohibited. While the most common caste system limited the noble class to rulers, advisors and priests, the Songhai empire gave great status to traders as well, allowing them to move freely in comparison to commoners.

The **Igbo** people of Nigeria practice the *Osu* caste system, which essentially only has two castes: "real born" and "outcast". Like other untouchable castes, the outcasts are treated as inferiors, not allowed to have real homes, and are not allowed to intermingle with the "real born". The origins of the system are shrouded in oral history; the most common stories say that the Osu were "living sacrifices", perhaps descended from people used for human sacrifice in ages past. Despite their pagan religious origins, the practice continued even after the peoples of the region adopted Christianity.

The **Wolof** people of Senegal divide their castes into two major groups. The freeborn, or *geer*, are at the top. This class includes nobility as well as landowning farmers. Below them are the *jaam* (slaves) and *nyenyo* (non-nobles), which includes woodworkers, leatherworkers, smiths and *griots*, who serve as musicians and historians. The jaam and nyenyo are essentially the same caste - the differences are only a matter of descent per se. The geer actually make up the large majority of the population, as opposed to the usual "nobles vs commoners" situation.

In **Hawaii**, there were four classes. Individuals were born into these classes and they could not be changed (except for losing rank and falling into the lowest). The four classes were *alii* (nobles), *kahuna* (priests), *maka'ainana* (commoners) and *kauwa* (outcasts). In Hawaiian law, a *kapu* was a taboo or law enforced primarily against commoners; breaking it meant death. Only nobles and priests had the power to create kapu, which gave them great power over the common class.

A simpler and more common subsection of caste separation is the divide between commoners and nobles, also known as "nobility". Nobility is a concept built on a fundamental difference of human value between low-born and high-born individuals. The high-born *nobility* have certain legal and social privileges that are denied to the low-born *commoners*, regardless of how much material wealth and power the commoners acquire. In some cases it is possible for a low-born individual to become a high-born, but depending on the system this may be extraordinary.

The governments of **China** went through many different periods with their own scales of "nobility" and "egalitarianism". There were certain periods of Chinese history that were considered "feudal", or *fengjian*. This includes the *Zhou* period and the later *Han* period. There were also periods that were more bureaucratic in nature, such as the *Qin* and *Song* periods. During the feudal periods, China did have a nobility (i.e. landowners in service to a king), but its privileges and hereditary status are sometimes unclear. For example, in the southern state of Chu during the Zhou period, "nobility" was solely bestowed as an award for service, and was not hereditary. When the first Emperor of China, Qin Shi Huang, succeeded in unifying the country, he eliminated all nobles and replaced their lands with administrative districts. The administrators of those districts were chosen on merit alone, making the country purely egalitarian in terms of birth. The Qin dynasty fell shortly after Qin Shi Huang's death, and out of the chaos rose warlords with their own loyal or paid followers. These warlords compensated their friends with lands and peasants, and thus a new feudal system was formed. It is notable that the ideology of Ruism/Confucianism overtly condemned "nobility of birth", instead celebrating "nobility of virtue". This attitude manifested itself in many ways during China's history, but that is not to say that it was always effective at fighting nepotism.

In classical **Athenian** society, there were "aristocrats" (*aristoi*) and commoners. This division was common throughout **Greece**. Originally the classes of rulership were open only to members of the aristoi, but with the reforms of Solon in the early 6th century BCE these requirements were removed. In addition, the distinct leadership positions were similarly discarded, replaced with direct democracy and assembly voting. Within the century, the aristoi and their birth value was nullified, replaced with a materialistic class system based on income. Despite this, Athens maintained a different sort of dualistic caste system: the difference between "citizens" and non-citizens (i.e. immigrants or freed slaves and their descendants). Citizen status was hereditary in nature; it was possible for non-citizens to be gifted citizenship, but rare. Citizens had many privileges and protections, such as protection from enslavement, that were coupled with their obligations of military service and democratic participation. In this way, the difference between citizens and non-citizens can be seen as its own split between nobles and non-nobles. In the *Hellenistic* period, however, it became common for non-citizens to be able to buy their way into citizenship; this redressed certain complaints, but the non-citizens still lacked a significant number of rights.

In the Republican era of **Rome**, the noble classes (*patricians* and *equites*) were separated from the common class (*plebians*). In the early Republic, the patricians were the only ones allowed to hold political office or priesthoods. They also had more votes in legislative assemblies. There were rich plebian families and poor patrician families, but nonetheless these privileges endured. The patricians' greed resulted in economic downturn for the plebians, which was opposed by populist reformers such as the Gracchi brothers. Eventually, political shifts and rebellions dethroned the patrician families, and their importance was vastly reduced. They were replaced by ambitious individuals from plebian families, such as Marcus Licinius Crassus, who eventually became the richest man in the republic. By the time of the empire, the ancient bloodlines were mostly unimportant in comparison to more direct forms of influence. This led the way to a more *egalitarian* approach, where power and wealth granted status all on their own.

In **Germanic** traditions, including that of the **Anglo-Saxons**, the word *ceorl* or *karl* designated a "free man" who was not a member of nobility (a king and their retainers, or *thegn*). Ceorls are originally depicted as being relatively free and swearing allegiance directly to their king, although the introduction of the feudal manoral system changed this. In early eras, the Anglo-Saxons made relatively few disinguishments between nobles and commoners, and there was a word - *gesithcund* - for a ceorl who owned enough land, and was outfitted with proper equipment, to be treated almost as a thegn. Depending on one's interpretation of the language, it may even have been possible for a ceorl's lineage to fully ascend to thegn status if they maintained their wealth over enough generations. This is described in *"The North Peoples' Law"*, a lawbook used to determine wergild and status.

Among the **Celts**, there is a difference between nobles and non-nobles, but sources are somewhat rare or scattered about the distinctions. In "The Gallic Wars", Julius Caesar describes the **Gauls** as having nobility who maintained severe control over non-nobles through debts of service. He also described power struggles between the nobles and the priesthood, or *druids*. The **Gaelic** culture split society into three main parts: the nobility (*nemed*), the commoners, and the "unfree", or slaves and serfs. The laws surrounding their division were documented in contemporary works such as *Bretha Nemed* and *Uraicecht Becc*. Similar to the Anglo-Saxon model, it was apparently possible for a commoner's line to become noble if they maintained certain requirements over several generations. Amongst the nobility, a distinction was drawn between landowning noble lords and landless nobles. The latter was based on one's profession; skilled craftsmen were included in it, as were scholars and poets (who maintained oral traditions and histories). A noble lord's status within their rank was dependent on the number of "clients" they had. "Client" here meant a subject, in a traditional feudal relationship - exchanging labor and service for protection, both military and legal. These bonds were made voluntarily, and on the death of a lord they had to be made anew to the lord's son (which was not automatic). Such a relationship may have been economically necessary, but it was still a "free choice", as opposed to serfdom.

During the reign of David I, the older Gaelic model of **Scotland** was replaced with a model more similar to Norman Feudalism. A text written during this time, "Laws of the Britons and Scots", distinguishes between noble families and those who are lower in status, called "churls" in the Anglo-Saxon way. David I's reforms also created a more solid noble class, who served as heavy cavalry similar to continental nobles, and encouraged castle-building across the country. These changes were partly done to improve Scotland's status among the other nations of Europe, by adhering more to their common model.

In **France**, the noble class was accorded certain privileges, gaining more and more until the tipping point of the French Revolution. A major component of French nobility was the *seigneurial system*, wherein the nobles could demand taxes and levies from commoners on their land. From the 15th century onwards, nobles were exempted from the *taille* land tax, used to pay for France's wars. These taxes were loathed by the common folk, but provided a substantial amount of income for the crown - about half its income in 1570, for example. Despite these perceived imbalances, the French nobility was not entirely impermeable. It was possible for a commoner to join the nobility by holding certain offices, such as a mayoral or military title. These were termed *noblesse de robe*, "nobility of the robe", in contrast with the blood-titled *noblesse de race* (nobility through breeding). It was also possible for a noble individual to lose their noble privileges, a process known as *dérogeance*. Such individuals would, for example, be forced to pay taxes on their land. This punishment was most commonly used on nobles who dabbled in mercantile pursuits, which was strictly discouraged.

In **Poland**, the noble class, or *szlachta*, had their own set of privileges. Due to Poland's electoral monarchy system, kings had a tendency to accord more and more rights to the szlachta in order to secure votes. For example, King Louis of Hungary made certain promises to the electorate so they would vote for his daughter, Jadwiga (who became the first Queen Regnant of Poland). These promises included release from tribute to the monarch (apart from a small consideration), release from construction duties (including castles, towns and bridges), payment of wages for military campaigns, and the restriction of high offices to those of Polish descent. In 1422, it was established that the king could not revoke a noble's lands unless the courts supported it. In 1496, the power of the nobility over their common folk was increased; serfs were prevented from leaving their lord's land, townsfolk were prohibited from owning land, and church positions were restricted to the nobility. It was *possible* for a commoner to earn a noble title, but between about 1400 and 1800, this only happened around 800 times. In short, the difference between noble and commoner was extremely solid, and eventually the powers of the nobility outstripped the powers of the king.

In *Edo* period **Japan**, there was a firm division between social classes. The strongest of these was between nobles (*daimyo*, lords, and *samurai*, retainers) and commoners. In the more tumultuous period of warring states (*Sengoku*), it was possible for a commoner to earn their way to a noble status by deed or force of arms. This was eliminated by Toyotomi Hideyoshi, who had himself arisen in just such a way. This was called the *mibun tōsei rei*, or "separation edict". It was accompanied by the *katanagari*, or "sword hunt", wherein all peasants were forcibly disarmed, leaving the samurai as the only armed class. Nobility had several classes of its own, with lower ranks highly deferential to upper ones, but the difference between the noble and the commoner was even more severe. This was most clearly represented by the *kiri-sute gomen*, or "right to cut and leave". This was a right possessed by samurai to kill a commoner (or anyone of lower class) who had offended them. There were restrictions on this right - it was not a free license to murder - but it was a definitive and lethal difference between the classes. The victim had the right to defend themselves with a short sword, but because of the disarmament, this right only applied in cases where a noble was offended by another noble of lower rank.

Among the cultures of the **Philippines**, there is a pan-regional nobility called the *Datu*. The specifics of their nature and control vary across the islands and the cultures represented on them. Among the **Visaya** people, the Datu were the first of a three-caste system; beneath them were the *Timawa*, or warriors, and then there were the common people, or *Oripun*. The Datu and Timawa were both hereditary castes who enjoyed legal principles over the common populace. The Datu were owed obedience and subservience from the Oripun beneath them. Lower-class Timawa had freedom of movement, and could choose their master as they pleased; higher-ranking Timawa were connected to a single ruler, but were exempt from taxation and farm service. The Timawa were somewhat strange in a hereditary sense in that their bloodline was connected to the Datu, as they were originally the illegitimate children of a Datu and a commoner. As such, these half-noble bastard children formed an intermediary caste between the other two.

In **Armenia**, a class of nobles called *nakharars* ("holders of the primacy") existed. They were similar in some ways to European nobility, in that they were single individuals with authority over a given region or estate. However, a notable difference is that such fiefdoms belonged to entire *families*, even though they were managed by one person at a time. What this means practically is that the family of the owner had their own rights concerning inheritance; for example, if a ruler died without an heir, the title would go to someone from a different branch of the family. The ruler could split his lands up only to give it to another member of the family, although a male ruler marrying outside the family would require a dowry of land given to the bride's family. For this reason, marriage among the nakharars was often endogamous within the family. This kept the land within the family, and tied into regional beliefs about positive incest (*xwēdōdah*).

4.3 Slavery and Serfdom

The institution of slavery is a relative constant for most of human history. However, there are some examples of cultures (or at least situations) where it has been outlawed or discouraged. In addition, not all slavery is made the same; some was "merely" reducing a person to the status of an indentured servant, while others were mired in dehumanization and abuse.

When the topic of slavery is brought up, what most modern people think of is <u>chattel slavery</u>. Chattel slavery involves the slave becoming the personal property of the owner, bought and sold as any other item, and treated accordingly. It was practiced in great numbers everywhere from Europe to the Middle East to Africa to Asia. The **Norse** were feared as prolific slave-traders, taking *thralls* in raids across Europe and often selling them to more cosmopolitan Muslim traders. Chattel slavery was dehumanizing by its very nature and was frequently associated with race, especially in later years. Chattel slaves were often taken in wars or raids, and if possible came from other religions or other ethnic groups.

In most cases, slaves lacked almost all rights and could be legally abused, raped or killed by their owners. However, this was not always true. The **Indian** king Ashoka produced a legal system called *Dhamma*, which included a statement that slaves should be treated as kindly as possible. Muslims and early Christians called for kindnesses in regards to the treatment of slaves, although slavery itself was normalized and deemed acceptable by both religions. Pre-Islamic **Iran** traditionally limited slavery *only* to prisoners-of-war and captured rebels, and furthermore had a great number of restrictions in place about how slaves could be treated. A document of the *Sassanid* period, the *Matikan-e-Hazar Datastan*, details the laws of slave-owning at the time. Violence against slaves was forbidden, slaves had to be given at least three days of rest a month, and a slave that converted to Zoroastrianism would be allowed to buy their own freedom.

In many cases, slaves were "bred", and their children would be slaves as well, leading to an unending chain of slavery often justified on racial grounds. This was not the case in **Greece**, according to evidence from the classical period; Xenophon advises slave-owners to keep their male and female slaves separate, as slave-children can cause unwanted problems of their own. Slavery in among the **Aztec** people was limited to individuals, and the children of slaves were born free. The act of *manumission*, or freeing one's slaves, was sometimes seen as virtuous. This was the case in **Rome, Iran**, and among Muslim cultures. However, the **Celts** actively discouraged it in their legal systems, and in **Greece** a freed slave would still retain many elements of an unfree status.

Another form of slavery is <u>debt bondage</u>, or bonded labor, which is also one of the most common forms of modern slavery. Debt bondage involves an individual owing money or resources to a debtor and working for them as a way to pay it off. The debt may be extended indefinitely, or the duration of the repayment may be indefinite, which means that this sort of labor can easily turn from a delayed exchange of goods and services to a form of inheritable slavery. Debt bondage was found among the **Greeks, Romans, Aztecs** and many more modern societies. When chattel slavery was banned, debt bondage tended to take its place - being a form of financial manipulation and entrapment, rather than a direct dehumanization.

Serfdom is sometimes considered a form of bonded labor. A serf was a contracted farmer who "belonged" to a feudal lord. In some cases, a serf had to voluntarily sign the freedom of their family line away, usually in exchange for protection (this contract would also affect all of his children, creating a serf class in perpetuity). In others, poor farmers were simply "taken" by a powerful lord because they were too weak to fight back. Serfs had a huge number of restrictions on their freedom based on their manorial contract - for example, being legally prevented from leaving their lands, as was the case in **Japan**'s Edo period or the **Roman Empire** after Constantine.

Serfdom was incredibly common across continental **Europe** and the **British Isles** in the early Middle Ages. The line between a serf and a true "slave" was often thin; the *kholops* of Russia were just below serfs in status, and they could be sold or even killed at whim by their masters. "Proper" serfs didn't fare much better. Serfdom generally replaced other forms of slavery. This was less true in Scandinavia, where slaves (*thralls)* were used in place of serfs. In many places serfs made up the vast majority of the population, with free commoners and nobles as the minority. Serfdom declined in Europe in the 14th century, partly as the result of the Black Death. The lowered population meant that commoners had a greater amount of leverage against the nobility (who still needed peasants around to grow food, after all), and thus serfdom became less common. However, in Eastern Europe, the pattern was reversed: serfdom was less common early on, and became more common after the 14th century, when many laws were enacted to restrict the rights of common folk.

In **Sparta**, the *helot* class was the only thing that allowed the free Spartan men to live their preferred warrior lifestyle. The helots were a class somewhere between slaves and serfs who (according to Herodotus) made up 7/8ths of the total population of Sparta. The helots were harshly mistreated by the Spartans, who lived in constant fear of uprisings due to their population difference. The helots lived on their own, without the direct control of an owner or overseer, but were periodically harassed or raided by their Spartan owners to keep them in line. Spartan boys would participate in an event called the *crypteia* when they reached the proper age; this involved living in the wild and terrorizing or murdering helots while escaping detection. The purpose of this event was twofold; firstly, to develop the killing instincts of the free Spartan, and secondly, as an ever-present menace to keep the helots in line.

The issue of abolitionism, or the outlawing of slavery, is dependent on the culture, the time period, and the type of slavery being outlawed. For example, the Catholic Church in the early Medieval period attempted to end the institution of slavery, but only of Christians. In some cases this condemnation extended to the enslavement of Muslims, but this was less successful. Similarly, Islam outlawed slavery of other Muslims. However, there were other, broader attempts at abolition throughout history. In **China**, the Qin, Ming and Qing dynasties each attempted to outlaw slavery, or at least serfdom, with limited results. The non-dynastic emperor Wang Mang also tried to ban slavery, but this lasted only three years. As mentioned prior, the **Iranian Empire** of Cyrus the Great essentially eliminated all slavery apart from prisoners-of-war, and even those slaves were required to be treated decently. In **Venice**, slavery was officially banned in the year 960, although the trade continued nonetheless. In the **Italian** city of Bologna, the *Liber Paradisus* of 1256 banned slavery and serfdom throughout the city and its holdings. In 1315, Louis X of **France** made slavery illegal on French ground and weakened the institution of serfdom - although the former would later be circumvented by French colonial interests in centuries to come. 20 years later, Magnus IV of **Sweden** outlawed slavery within the borders of his country, which created similar colonial loopholes.

Enslaved peoples would also sometimes take their freedom into their own hands, by way of <u>slave revolts</u>. Slave revolts generally had two forms. In the first, slaves would take up arms in order to try to fight their way out of their captors' reach, thus earning their own freedom. In the second, slaves would attempt to dismantle slavery itself as a whole. The former were much more common than the latter for practical reasons, but the latter sticks more for ideological ones. For example, the gladiator rebellion of Spartacus (the *Third Servile War*) was sometimes romanticized as a fight for freedom, but was generally more about *individual* freedom than the concept itself. The slaves under Spartacus really just wanted to go home; their only other consistent motivation was raiding and plundering Roman cities.

In contrast, the *Zanj Rebellion* had more organized goals. This was a rebellion in 9th century **Iraq** of **Ethiopian** slaves against **Arab** Muslim masters; the name comes from the Arabic word for **Ethiopians**, which most of the slaves were. The slaves had been worked brutally to harvest sugarcane, despite Muslim tenets about kind treatment of slaves. Under leadership of Ali ibn Muhammad, an enigmatic figure who claimed descent from the fourth caliph of Islam, the Zanj fought off their masters so effectively that they essentially established their own country. This new country was complete with taxation and their own minted currency - in effect, they controlled proper territory as a governing body. However, they were only able to achieve that much because the Abbasid Caliphate of the time was in a period of turmoil and chaos; once it had reorganized itself, the Zanj were put down brutally.

Most slave-owning societies recognized that their slaves desired freedom, even as they denied it to them. One interesting divergence from this is **American** slavery; in the early 19th century, there were many institutions attempting to make the argument that the slaves were happy in chains, and were too simple to care about freedom. The theory of *drapetomania* was posited by Samuel Cartwright as a mental illness that made slaves want to run away, indicating that subservience was part of their "normal condition". Pro-slavery propaganda of the time suggested that all African people really wanted was cheap pleasures like watermelon, not anything as complex as freedom. This is partly why watermelon has racist connotations even today; the other reason is that watermelon is eaten in a messy, undignified manner, which is also why fried chicken was associated with Africans. These attitudes were used to morally justify slavery, and for this reason their legacy continued even after slavery itself was banned.

V. AUTHORITY & GOVERNANCE

Once a society has been organized into a larger form of government, the issue becomes "who will be in charge of that government?" Whether it's a charismatic or powerful individual who takes charge and establishes a dynasty, a religious organization that rules in the name of a god, or the people themselves cooperating to get things done, *someone* has to be in charge.

5.1 Autocratic Governments

One of the most common government types in the pre-modern world is the *autocracy*, or *rule by one*. This includes hereditary autocracies such as kingdoms or empires as well as dictatorships established on other lines. In some cases a government is ostensibly autocratic but has influences from council elements, such as a constitutional monarchy or an electoral monarchy.

The most common form of kingly descent is <u>hereditary</u>. That is to say, the crown passes automatically from blood to blood, based on the laws and traditions in place. There are several ways for titles to pass. Hereditary inheritance could be *agnatic*, in which case only men were eligible, it could be *agnatic-cognatic*, in which case the title could go to a woman if an appropriate man was not available, or in rare cases it could be fully *cognatic*, in which case it would go to the best candidate regardless of sex.

In *primogeniture*, in which the eldest surviving child of the monarch takes all titles. This had the effect of keeping the title united, rather than fragmenting it at the death of every monarch. In some cases a lord would grant their other sons lands before their death, to ensure their status after the eldest's inheritance. Governments that practiced primogeniture included the **English**, the **French** (under *Salic* law), the **Holy Roman Empire** (for titles lower than Emperor), **Brittany**, **Burgundy**, and so on. The **Basque** people of Navarre practiced cognatic primogeniture, meaning that all titles went to the oldest child, whether that child was male or female.

In *partible inheritance*, titles are distributed amongst claimants; this was practiced by the **Germans**, **Norwegians**, **Franks**, **Rus**, **Welsh** and **Chinese** in varying ways. Partible inheritance would weaken individual states, but would guarantee a stronger inheritance for each claimant. For example, the Kingdom of the **Franks** was split in 768, when King Pepin was succeeded by Charles (who received the north) and Carloman (who received the south). Carloman eventually retired from politics under questionable circumstances, leaving Charles the sole ruler - later to become Charles the Great, or Charlemagne.

Partible inheritance was sometimes tied to the idea that a family, not a patriarch or matriarch, "owned" the land; this was the case in the Germanic system of *"Salic patrimony"*. The core idea was also shared by the previously-mentioned **Armenian** *nakharar* class, although inheritance was not always "split". In **China**, partible inheritance was relatively common, with primogeniture being limited to the early periods of the northern regions. Partible inheritance was sometimes used as a way to control powerful families by splitting their holdings amongst multiple sons.

One example of partible inheritance comes from **Norway**; after the death of King Harald III, his realm was split between the north, under Magnus II, and the south, under Olaf III. Notably, Olaf was on campaign his father when he died in battle, and for this reason Magnus ruled alone for roughly three months until Olaf returned to claim his half.

Among the **Inca**, the belief in the divine spirit of kings led to a particular custom, which was the idea that the kings needed to maintain their own lands even after death. When a king died he was mummified; the lands he had conquered were given to the junior family dynasty, or *panaqas*, for them to govern in his name. The senior family dynasty (the king's eldest son) received the power and title of rulership, but the lands conquered by the previous king were not his. This gave each new king impetus to conquer his own domain outside of the empire. However, it also gave the panaqas a great deal of power, rivaling the king's own. This system was called *split inheritance*, and was unique to their culture.

In *seniority*, the crown passes to the monarch's brother, and eventually cousins. This was used in the *Alaouite* dynasty of **Morocco**, the *Zagwe* dynasty of **Ethiopia**, and the modern ruling house of **Saudi Arabia**. The *rota system* was a system used by the **Kievan Rus**, in which succession would pass from brother to brother. Once the brothers were exhausted, the line would pass to the eldest son of the eldest of those brothers, and then continue anew. The originator of this system was Yaroslav the Wise, who used it to quell concerns of dissent amongst his five surviving sons.

Among the **Nair** people of Kerala, India, there was a form of succession called *marumakkathayam*. This form favored matrilineal descent, which fit with the female-centric layout of their society. In the 18th century Kingdom of **Travancore**, which was founded in that area, this succession was agnatic in nature. The succession order was thus: first, the brothers of the current ruler, from the same mother. If none were available, it would go to the sons of his eldest sister down to the youngest. From there, it would go to his cousins by his mother's sisters, again going from oldest sister to youngest. It would never pass from father to son, and yet only men could inherit.

An alternative to automatic hereditary descent was an electoral monarchy. In these systems, the monarch still held major power and, often, divine importance. However, the assignment of kingly status was given to others, either "the people as a whole" or a smaller, oligarchic group.

Amongst the **Germanic** peoples, kings were chosen by the free peoples of their tribe. Viable candidates had to be connected by blood to the tribe's founder, and kingship had a religious or divine element to it. The historian Tacitus noted that kings were "chosen by birth", and their power would vary between nations. This sort of "king elected by all peoples" succession was also used in **Sweden** until the mid-1500s. A similar model was used by the **Gaelic** peoples of Ireland and the **Picts** of Scotland, although the Gaels limited blood descent to the male line, whereas the Picts accepted bloodlines descended from both men and women.

An alternative to this is election-by-nobility, wherein only those who hold certain noble positions are allowed to vote. This was the practice in the **Holy Roman Empire**, where the Emperor was chosen by the *prince-electors*. In the oldest traditions there were seven electors: three

James Shea

bishops and four high-ranking nobles. In **Poland**, after the elimination of the Piast dynasty, kings were elected by the Polish noble class, or *szlachta*. A similar arrangement existed in the African kingdom of **Kongo**, among the **Yoruba** people, and in the **Mali** empire.

In the **Muslim** world, the original four *caliphs*, or supreme religious leaders, were elected by a *shura*, or council of leaders. In the case of the third caliph's election, for example, the shura consisted of five men, including the man who would become the caliph. This eventually transitioned into the hereditary *Umayyad Caliphate* after a tumultuous period. *Sunni* Muslims believe that those first four caliphs are the legitimate successors of Muhammad, while *Shia* Muslims believe the succession should have gone to his cousin and (they believe) designated successor, Ali.

Among certain **Gallic** peoples, such as the **Aedui**, a title called the *vergobret* was used as a temporary king or chieftain. The vergobret was elected by the druidic class every year, and was given many powers in pursuit of defending his tribe. However, he was not allowed to leave his people's territory, and thus could not lead the military on offensive campaigns. This kept him under the watchful eyes of the druids, unable to exploit his position for greater power.

For some governments succession was determined by the <u>ruler's preference</u>. If done well, by a wise leader, this could lead to a succession of intelligent and capable leaders. In other cases, it could lead to favoritism and nepotism.

Amongst the **Roman** emperors, succession was meant to be based on the current emperor's choice. In the period of the "Five Good Emperors", the emperor would adopt his chosen successor, passing along his title on merit and intelligence. This produced a good, solid succession of wise leaders. The last of these, Marcus Aurelius, named his own son Commodus as emperor instead of adopting on merit. Commodus was a more vain and arbitrary ruler who was eventually assassinated (by strangulation in a bath), and after his death the Senate declared him a public enemy of the state. His death was followed by the year of five emperors, a massive civil war fought by powerful claimants.

The first three emperors of **China** were purportedly part of a succession-by-merit system. The ancient sage-king Yao was a legendary figure, praised by later generations as morally pure and highly intelligent. Yao was unhappy with his own sons and passed his mantle onto Shun, a minister who had impressed Yao with his diligence and success. Yao married Shun to two of his own daughters, and when Yao retired, Shun took the throne. Shun ruled capably until he was 100 years old. Shun was succeeded by his own chosen heir, Yu, who had similarly impressed the Emperor with his capability. When Yu died, his own son Qi took the throne, thus ending the system of appointment-by-merit. This made Yu the first king of the *Xia* dynasty, and Qi the second.

A ruler designating multiple successors in their will seemed to be a reasonable possibility in Early Medieval **Spain**, in opposition to systems where inheritance was more "automatic". An example was the division of the realms of Sancho III of Pamplona, who controlled the Catholic realms of northern Spain. Before his death, Sancho split his holdings amongst his sons, creating the Kingdoms of Pamplona, Aragon and Leon (as well as one smaller territory for another son). These brothers feuded over their inheritance, leading to open confrontation and bloodshed. The King of Leon, Ferdinand I, gained the largest territory. In his will, he split his holdings between his three sons and two daughters; the sons gained the roughly equal-sized holdings of Galicia, Leon and Castille, while the daughters each received a city. Again, Ferdinand's sons fought over the throne, and his son Alfonso VI of Leon became King of all their territories. Alfonso VI would have chosen his own son to succeed him, but his son died early, forcing him to leave the throne to his daughter, Urraca. Urraca ruled as Queen Regnant because her own husband had died before she took the throne (meaning she didn't have to cede power to him), and her sole son eventually took total power as Alfonso VII. This newest Alfonso eventually split his lands between his two sons, but one of those sons died shortly after taking power, resulting in a shift to a more direct single-inheritor system.

Many autocratic governments are simply taken by force; such governments are often called dictatorships. Such governments are uncommon in the pre-modern era. Rather, coups and rebellions took hold of existing power structures, such as kingly titles, which gave them cultural and religious legitimacy. Still, there are occasional examples of governments that existed purely on the ruler's power, and also some examples of governments where "taking power by force" was an accepted and legal method of succession.

In 83 BC, the **Roman** politician Lucius Sulla essentially conquered his own city, killing his enemies and filling the senate with his supporters. He was named "dictator", a position that was normally a temporary position for emergency measures. However, Sulla's power was considered to be without a time limit, and he radically changed the Roman government in that time period to accommodate his needs. He resigned only three years later due to other pressures. Thirty years later, the same title was passed to Julius Caesar, who was on the verge of creating a similarly limitless position before he was murdered by Republic-supporting opponents.

In the **Greek** world, certain rulers are remembered as *tyrants,* who took power through a combination of force and popularity. For example, the **Athenian** Peisistratos who took control of the republic with popular support from the lower classes. Once in power he weakened the rich in ways considered humiliating to them, which improved his standing amongst the poor. Peisistratos was undoubtedly a tyrant because his power stemmed from physical force, not legal means, and rested solely in himself. However, he used his reign to try to improve the government and ease tensions between the classes. Both Herodotus and Aristotle remembered him relatively fondly. However, his aristocratic rivals forced him out of office several times, leading to three separate reigns. Less popular were tyrants such as Cleisthenes of **Sicyon**, Periander of **Corinth**, and Peisistratos' son Hippias. These tyrants may have had positive effects but were generally perceived to be cruel or arbitrary in a position they had not legally "earned".

In the *open succession* of the early **Ottoman Empire**, the concept of "taking control by force" was an intentional design choice. A Sultan's sons - all of them - would be accorded provinces while the Sultan was alive. Upon the Sultan's death, the sons would fight each other for control. A Sultan could indicate preference based on the province they gave to their son; the Sultan's many wives also affected the process by supporting their sons through intrigue. Eventually, this led to a system where succession was smoother and more like primogeniture; however, this was accompanied by mass fratricide, as the new Sultan killed all his potential rivals. Later, this was replaced again; the Sultan's brothers were sent to live in luxury in the harems, where they wielded no political powers and thus posed no threat.

The Imperial seat of **China** was generally hereditary primogeniture, going to the emperor's eldest son, or brother if they had no sons. However, there was a principle called the *tiānmìng*, or "Mandate of Heaven". This principle stated that an emperor's right to rule was given to them by heaven, and was self-evident in nature. If a dynasty survived, it was meant to do so; if it fell, it was meant to do that. As a result, taking the imperial throne by force was common in Chinese history, even by commoners (as happened with the Han and Ming dynasties). It justified rebellion, or at least *successful* rebellion, and gave emperors incentive to stay popular amongst their subjects.

5.2 Councils & Communes

Not all societies were ruled by a dominant individual. Many societies cooperated together more equitably, making decisions that included some, or even all, of society in the process. Some societies took it even further, seeking full equality between all members of society.

Unlike an autocratic government, a council government includes the voices of several representatives. These voices can be limited to noble families (an *oligarchy*), or in some cases they can represent all citizens. Council governments can have an elected leader, but that leader lacks the overriding power of a true autocracy.

The **Greek** city-states (or *polis*) were often republics, although kingdoms or (usually temporary) dictatorships were also possible. In **Corinth**, the ruling council was originally confined to the ruling Bacchidae clan, headed by an elected figurehead, the *prytanis*. The city-state of **Chalcis** is recorded as having an aristocratic rule, which was overthrown by the Athenians and replaced with a colonial government. The government of **Syracuse** alternated between tyrants and democratic rule (which was usually temporary - tyrants would be overthrown by the people, and the people would hold power until a new tyrant came in). **Athens** was originally controlled by several *archons* (three to nine) who ruled with the help of a council of noble family members. The lower classes were intentionally excluded from the proceedings, making the government an oligarchic one in nature.

In medieval **Italy**, there was a resurgence of the city-state system, usually semi-oligarchic in nature (i.e. permitting only the participation of noble families). These were called the *maritime republics*. Their governments tended to be tumultuous, characterized by coups or conquests in a manner similar to the Greek city-states. Maritime republics were frequently ruled by a *doge*, or duke, who was elected by vote. Unlike a "noble" duke, however, doges had many checks and balances in their roles, making them closer to a president in nature. Candidates for doge were almost always supported by merchant families, and if their candidate won, it essentially meant a victory for the family at large.

In **Venice**, the vote was limited to around forty electors, although the number waxed and waned. The doge position was for life, although the doge was under constant surveillance to prevent misdeeds. It was unacceptable, for example, for a Venetian doge to open foreign correspondence without other officials present. More broadly, there was a council of around 2000 noblemen who voted on important issues facing the city-state. In **Genoa**, the doge title was originally elected by popular vote amongst all citizens, and the position was similarly for life. In 1528 it was turned into a two-year position elected by a small council of nobles. In general, the doges of Genoa had less power than those of Venice. The city-state of **Amalfi** was originally ruled by elected *prefects*, and then *patricians*, until settling on the title of "duke".

The *free imperial cities* of the **Holy Roman Empire** were technically under an elective monarchy system. However, they were "free" in that their own republican governments reported directly to the Emperor, rather than being ruled by an intermediate noble. Similar arrangements existed in antiquity, such as **Athens** under **Roman** rule (beginning with Emperor Hadrian).

In the **Icelandic Commonwealth**, which existed from 930 to 1262 CE, government was composed of elected chiefs, or *goðar* (pronounced "gothar"). There were 36 goðar, split into four districts. A goðar was supported by their voters, or "assembly people", who received protection and support in exchange for their votes and military service. A citizen could pledge support to any of the nine chiefs within their district. Each goðar also appointed a judge, and the 36 judges formed the judicial branch of the government. There was occasional conflict between goðar, using their supporters as soldiers. However, these battles were small in scale and had low casualty rates. In general, Iceland was thought to be more peaceful than many nearby regions of the era.

Poland was an elective monarchy through most of its existence. In 1569, the king had ceded so much power to his nobles that they essentially overrode him as a power in the country. King Alexander I Jagiellon signed an act that said the king could not pass a law without the consent of the nobles. In short, the nobles controlled the lawmaking process. This noble-run government was termed the *Rzeczpospolita*, meaning "common thing" (sometimes translated as "commonwealth"). It was a council-run state, but one with a very strict and near-inviolable distinction between the highly-empowered nobility and the rights-deprived common folk. For this reason it is sometimes called a "republic of nobles".

The **Haudosaunee Confederacy** of the American Northeast was composed of six tribes. The confederacy itself was run by the "Grand Council of the Six Nations", composed of 56 chiefs (*hoyenah*), as well as a council of the tribe's mothers. Any decision or treaty had to pass through both groups with supermajority approval (the required amount depended on the subject). In addition, male leaders were chosen by their clan's mothers, and could be demoted if they displeased them. It was, in essence, a government built on community consensus that included both men and women.

Some cultures dispensed entirely with the idea of noble representatives, even elected ones, and simply ruled themselves by communal agreement. There were varying degrees of this. One form was the democratic assembly, wherein a society would be composed of freemen living their own lives who would come together for purposes of voting or communal action.

As mentioned earlier, **Athens** was originally ruled by a noble council of archons. In 594 BCE, the reformer Solon took power; under him, the system was opened to include all citizens (i.e. adult male landowners) regardless of wealth. Officials were chosen by a process called *sortition*, which was essentially random. However, these officials merely oversaw the process itself; most decisions were made by direct democracy, with voting done at an assembly, or *ecclesia*. Attending an assembly was considered essentially mandatory; during meetings, a police force of slaves would stalk the city looking for absentees. If they found one, they would lash them with a red-stained rope, which would leave red marks on their clothing identifying them as truant.

The **Rus** people occasionally used a form of assembly called a *veche*. Some sources indicate that it actually predates the Rus people, being derived from tribal assemblies, but it is the Rus who give us the most documentation of it. It was used most notably in the **Republic of Novgorod**, where it became the highest legislative court in the land after a princely ruler was overthrown in 1136. The Novgorod veche involved all citizens of the city; it was used for the election of roles such as mayors and *tysyatskies*, which was a complex role that combined a representative of the common man, a military leader, and an ambassador. The documents detailing the veche process often differ, and some historians have argued that it was merely a formality for a more oligarchic form of rule.

Among the **Oromo** people of Ethiopia, a practice called *gadaa* was sometimes used. Gadaa was essentially a form of public assembly and voting that was sectioned by class. Every eight years, a meeting called the *Gumi Gayo* would be convened, and laws would be voted on at this meeting. A leader called an *Abba Gada* would be elected, and his power would last until the next Gumi Gayo. However, the votes made at such assemblies were segregated; women were not allowed to vote at all, and class and ethnicity affected the strength of one's vote.

In **Scandinavian** and **Germanic** societies, an assembly called a þing ("thing") was held periodically to mediate issues between clans or tribes. While most groups generally had an elected king as described earlier, the þing represented an opportunity for communal voting and participation, watched over by officials called "lawspeakers". While the most important families generally swayed the vote, in theory the þing was a purely democratic affair. The relationship between the people and the kings was a two-way affair well into the medieval period. In 1018, King Olof Skötkonung of **Sweden** was vexed by the willfulness of his subjects, until he was reminded by a lawspeaker that a king's power was dependent on the freemen and their vote.

Furthermore, the lawspeaker went so far as to make direct threats to the king, saying that five previous Swedish kings had been killed by their angry subjects. At this point, the king relented to the will of the community.

Beyond the core democratic assembly, there was a more intense level of communalism. Communalism was built both on equality and cooperation, with shared resources and wealth between them. Communal movements tended to be temporary, and were often crushed as a threat by larger governments.

Because of certain interpretations of early *Christian* doctrine (such as the idea of *koinonia*, all things in common), communalism is common among certain Christian groups. The *Taborites* of **Bohemia**, one of several 15th century *Hussite* sects, were a radical Christian community centered on the town of Tábor. The Taborites attempted to build a classless communal society within their town, and thanks to bountiful gold mines nearby they managed to hold their own for a while. They operated under a principle called "Nothing is mine, nothing is yours, everything is common to all". A prospective citizen would give up all their possessions to join, but once they did so they would be taken care of by the community. Equal rights were granted to men and women, and religious ceremonies were designed to be inclusive of all (as opposed to Catholic ceremonies, which put more power in the hands of the priests). The various Hussite sects survived Imperial German invasions and Catholic crusades; however, once these outside threats were taken care of, the disparate sects eventually destroyed each other at the *Battle of Lipany*. The survivors, recognizing their weakness, all acceded to the control of Sigismund the Holy Roman Emperor. Sigismund himself commented on this, saying that "the Bohemians could be overcome only by Bohemians".

Another German communalist was Thomas Müntzer. A contemporary of Protestant leader Martin Luther, Müntzer was more committed to class equality than Luther, and clashed with him on issues of feudal authority. Müntzer became a leader of the **German Peasants' War** of 1524-1525. The movement was motivated by the increasing rights of the nobility in contrast to the decreasing rights of the peasants; the nobility had taken over previously-common land, and in addition heavy taxes were levied on the peasants by the nobility. The rebel forces were governed by "rings", democratic community circles where tactics and policies were discussed. There was a chain of command, with appointed marshals and officers, but it was loose when compared to their Imperial enemies. However, in comparison to the earlier Hussite wars, the German peasants were overcome by artillery and heavy cavalry, neither of which they possessed in great numbers. The peasants were eventually scattered; Müntzer was tortured and executed.

Other Christian movements with communalist branches include the *Waldensians* (originally the "Poor Men of Lyons"), *Anabaptists*, and *Puritans*. Communalists were often persecuted as heretics (by the church) or rebels (by the nobility), leading to exile or atrocities such as the Piedmont Easter - a massacre so brutal that it was widely condemned throughout Europe.

In **Iran**, the *Zoroastrian* prophet Mazdak was an activist and proto-socialist who lived in the 5th and early 6th centuries CE. Mazdak's ideology - naturally termed *Mazdakism* - preached pacifism, free love and social equality through shared possessions. While he was never able to put his design into full effect, he did have the ear of King Kavadh I, who put many social programs into effect. However, Kavadh was eventually chased from power by hostile nobles of his court, and while he did return, his fear of another uprising led him to distance himself from Mazdak. As a result, Mazdak and his followers were put to death by Kavadh's son, Khosrow.

The *Muslim* faith has a history of socialist aspects, at least in certain branches. The oldest adherent of such an aspect is Abū Dhar al-Ghifari, one of the prophet's original companions. Abū protested the excesses of the rich and preached redistribution of wealth. After Mohammed's death, many of his followers were tempted by the wealth they had accumulated, and Abū spent much of his time attempting to convince them of their error. This brought him into conflict with the Caliph,

Uthman, who was himself rich, and given to distributing war loot among powerful companions. Despite this, there is a long tradition of charitable giving in Islam, and the first Caliph - Uthman's predecessor, Abu Bakr - instituted a guaranteed income for all citizens. In later years, under the Caliph Umar, these programs were broadly expanded, and any indulgence in luxuries by those in power was condemned. In this way, the Caliphate at many points could be considered a "welfare state" of sorts, even if its governance was never communal in nature. It is perhaps notable that Muslim governments treated their Muslim citizens well because they heavily taxed non-Muslims under their jurisdiction. In some cases, such as that of governor Al-Hajjaj ibn Yusuf, non-Muslims were prevented from converting to Islam in order to preserve the region's economy.

5.3 Centralization & Independence

In addition to determining the type of government, another key issue when discussing governance is how centralized that government is, versus how divided it is. In essence, this issue is about how much power (legal and practical) is wielded by the leader of a government versus how much power is wielded by his ostensible subordinates or vassals.

The two primary forms of delegation were the feudal system (where a family or dynasty was granted lands of their own, with obligations that accompanied it) and the governor system (where an individual was appointed as an administrator only as a representative of the ruler). Both feudal lords and governors have participated in rebellions and civil wars throughout history. However, the former were generally more powerful and entitled than the latter, and wielded more material and legal power.

In the history of **England**, there were several *Barons' Wars* where feudal vassals militarily challenged the authority of their king. Prior to the *First Barons' War*, King John of England had been forced to sign a document - the *Magna Carta* - that granted more rights to his vassals. However, he refused to abide by the terms established, and as a result many nobles rebelled against him. The goal of these rebellious barons was to install Louis of France (later King Louis VIII) on the English throne, based on his maternal lineage. The rebels were eventually defeated and Louis relinquished his claims. The *Second Barons' War* took place fifty years later, and was a more conventional rebellion. The English King, Henry III, had been pressured into re-affirming the Magna Carta, as well as signing the *Provisions of Oxford*, which created a council of barons that would limit the king's power. However, Henry obtained permission from the Pope to disregard that document, and as a result was able to legally wage war against the rebels. The rebel leader, Simon de Montfort, appointed both nobles and non-nobles to his advisory council, and was functionally the head of a parliamentary government. However, the rebels were defeated at the Battle of Evesham in 1265. Still, the struggle between the king and his vassals continued throughout history - in another 50 years, the *Ordinances of 1311* would once again restrict the power of the king, and lead to yet another rebellion (the *Despenser War*).

In 1485, **France** became embroiled in a civil war called the *Mad War*. After the death of King Louis XI, his son Charles VIII was not yet old enough to take the throne. Therefore, his sister Anne de Beaujeu served as his regent alongside her husband, Duke Peter II of Bourbon. They faced opposition from Louis II of Orleans, the late king's cousin, alongside many other dukes and lesser nobles. The loyalist forces made use of the armies of loyal nobles as well as the central "royal" army in order to quell the rebellion. While the rebel dukes were defeated, they were subjected to punishing measures, but most were not killed or imprisoned for the sake of the country's stability. The leader of the rebellion, Louis II, even managed to inherit the throne ten years later as Louis XII of France. This signifies that even rebellious feudal vassals, who had committed high treason against the crown, still had a strong legal values and protections on them. Compared to a governor's position, an inherited feudal title had a more complicated relationship between lord and subject.

As discussed, the nobility of **Poland** - the *szlachta* - historically held a large amount of control over the country and the monarch. At the beginning of the 17th century, King Zygmunt III reasserted the crown's control over the realm by attempting to institute measures to weaken the nobility. He even attempted to destroy the elected monarch and replace it with a hereditary one. The nobles revolted, leading to *Zebrzydowski's Rebellion*. This rebellion was legally justified as outlined in the *Privilege of Mielnik*. Royalist forces won the war (which was relatively bloodless), and the power of the nobility was reduced. However, this was done by solidifying the country's legal system, which also reduced attempts to increase the power of the monarchy. Other rebellions like this, called *rokosz*, were common in Polish history. Some never even reached combat, such as the satirically-named *wojna kokosza*, or "*Chicken War*", of 1537. Others were more serious, such as *Lubomirski's Rebellion* in 1665.

In **China**, the process of centralization and decentralization was a constant battle throughout history. As mentioned in section 4.2, China changed several times from a feudal landlord system to a centralized bureaucracy system. The first time this happened was during the unification of China under the *Qin* dynasty. Dukes and barons became governors and administrators under the authority of the Imperial government, and these officials were chosen by merit and loyalty rather than by hereditary right. When the bureaucracy broke down, the wealthiest or most powerful bureaucrats declared their own sovereignty, and the feudal system re-opened. For the Qin dynasty, this breakdown was represented by the *Dazexiang Uprising* (209 BCE), which led to the *Chu-Han Contention* (206-202 BCE) which led to the rise of the new *Han* dynasty. The later Tang dynasty created a similar bureaucracy, which was more long-lived, but ultimately broke down after 300 years, leading to the *Five Dynasties and Ten Kingdoms Period* (907-979 CE). There were also several "warring states" periods in China's history, such as the *Spring And Autumn Period* (771-476 BCE) and the *Three Kingdoms Period* (220-280 CE) that were the result of a feudal system breaking down.

A feudal breakdown was also the cause of **Japan's** *Era of Warring States*. While the Divine Emperor was the theoretical ruler of the country, the practical ruler was his head general, the *Shogun*. However, the power of the Shogun weakened, and the lords under him became emboldened by the Shogunate's weakness in dealing with several rebellions. As a result, the country became a free-for-all between the various lords of the country. The Emperor and Shogun both existed only as figureheads. The ruling Shogun was assassinated, and his heir was used by the lord Oda Nobunaga as a bartering chip to establish his own legitimacy. Years of warring between lords occurred, followed by a short period of unification and then a civil war between parts of the newly unified country. After the civil war was won, its victor Tokugawa Ieyasu was appointed the new Shogun, and asserted the power of his office to maintain stability for the next few centuries. Part of this stability involved levying greater control over the noble houses - but not so great that they would arise again in revolt.

In the original **Iranian** Empire under Cyrus the Great, the Empire as a whole was split into provinces, governed by twenty-six *satraps*. In his own function, a satrap was not necessarily different from a vassal king or duke; he collected taxes for his territory, and served as the chief judge of the region he administered. One important difference between a satrap and earlier models of division was that the earlier model gave some level of "divine right to rule" to the vassal ruler, whereas a satrap did not have that privilege. A satrap administered his region through the grace of his emperor. Many of his advisors reported directly to the emperor, including his secretary, financial officer, and the general of the local army. However, the satraps were allowed to have a limited military force of their own (used to patrol roads and keep the peace) as well as having their own income from taxation and land-owning. This material power meant that when the authority of the emperor broke down, the satraps were often able to rise up and assert their independence. In 366 BCE, the *Great Satraps' Revolt* pitted several rebellious satraps against Artaxerxes II, who commanded his royal armies and loyal satraps against them.

The various provinces of the **Roman** Empire were administered by governors appointed by the emperor or by the senate. The emperor-appointed governors controlled "Imperial provinces", and worked under the emperor's direct authority. Senate-appointed governors were sent to "public provinces", which were held ostensibly by the Roman people. Such governors were often senators themselves. Imperial provinces were usually on the "exterior" of the Empire, while Senate provinces were on the "interior" - safer regions where military power was less important. Imperial governors had the authority to command legions, which was necessary for their role, while senate governors lacked this ability. When Rome had its own periods of warfare, such as the *Year of Five Emperors* (193 CE) or the *Crisis of the Third Century* (235-284 CE), the contenders involved were usually governors who used their positions to leverage local power.

VI. CRAFTS & ECONOMICS

A society is defined partly by the resources it has access to. A society's resources affect the way they live and the things they are capable of. Before we can talk about material aspects of culture, such as art or fashion or cuisine, it is necessary to establish where the components and materials came from.

6.1 Gathering, Farming & Herding

Human beings began as animals - as bipedal, intelligent apes
scavenging and hunting to survive. The difference between *homo
sapiens* and other living things was their ability to control and shape
their environment. For some cultures, simply surviving (or *subsisting*)
was good enough. However, others developed more complex systems
that allowed for greater growth, both in numbers and in technology.

Hunter-Gatherers were the original human model of subsistence; as the
name suggests, hunter-gatherers obtain food and items through the
immediate act of *taking* it, rather than cultivating or sowing. A
hunter-gatherer's diet includes meat from wild animals, fish, shellfish,
berries, nuts, fruit, mushrooms, and wild vegetables. All of these food
types, naturally, are also eaten by more developed peoples as well,
albeit as an addition to their more "staple" diet options.
Hunter-gatherer groups tend to be fully nomadic, roaming from place
to place based on the availability of seasonal plants or game.

Hunter-gatherer societies have several interesting traits that are worth
discussion. Firstly, hunter-gatherers tend to be more egalitarian than
more developed societies, both in terms of class division and in terms
of sexual equality. There are rarely hereditary or even lifelong leaders,
and the small number of available resources means that inequality in
that field is unlikely. The only social distinction made is that men
generally hunt, while women generally gather, although there are
exceptions to this (such as the Filipino **Aeta** peoples, the South African
Jul'hoan peoples, and the Australian **Martu** peoples. Secondly, life in
a hunter-gatherer society was relatively pleasant. Anthropologist
Marshall Sahlins presented data suggesting that hunter-gatherers
worked less than more developed peoples, had more leisure time, and
ate relatively well. The biggest difference was that hunter-gatherers did
not expect much out of life other than what they had, and thus were
more easily satisfied.

The downside of a hunter-gatherer society is that it leaves little room
for serious improvements. This is due to the lack of a food surplus.

Since every individual is engaged in keeping themselves (and their families) fed, there can be no "specialized" professions such as full-time crafters or builders. While hunter-gatherers do have some influence on their environment, such as forest gardens (essentially the protection of beneficial wild plants), they ultimately lacked the development necessary to truly change their surroundings.

Pastoral Nomadic societies are what happens when a cultural group develops animal domestication and husbandry, but not farming. Pastoral nomads lead herds of animals around from pasture to pasture, allowing the animals to eat what they can and moving when food becomes scarce. This is in contrast to sedentary agriculture, which relies upon growing food for both humans and animals to eat. Pastoral nomads are common in less-fertile areas, such as steppes and tundra, which is less valuable to sedentary agricultural societies. Horses are very important to many pastoral nomadic societies, as their improved mobility contributes greatly to their ability to manage large herds and move from place to place. Such societies are called *horse cultures*, and they have a larger percentage of riders than sedentary cultures of similar size.

Nomadic societies are not constantly mobile, but tend to linger in an area for a span ranging from half a year to a few years. The **Mongols**, for example, tend to have "summer locations" and "winter locations" (usually caves or other protected places to shelter animals during the winter). Herding adds a great deal of technological and developmental potential to a culture, when compared to hunter-gatherers. Domesticated animals offer resources and materials in larger, more reliable numbers compared to hunting. However, there is an upper ceiling of sorts on nomadic technology. Metalworking, for example, is difficult due to a lack of deep mines as well as a limit on the size of forges. In essence, if it can't be packed up and moved, it doesn't work for a nomadic culture. Small, portable forges could be placed on animal-drawn wagons or carts, but larger forges or facilities did not have that option.

<u>Sedentary</u> peoples are agricultural in nature. In contrast to nomads, sedentary societies are built around developing a single area into a habitable zone over a long period of time. This process includes clearing land for farming or grazing, building shelters, houses and storage areas, and fortifying those settlements. Sedentary societies become attached to a certain portion of territory and the food that can be grown in it. This makes them more vulnerable to localized disasters (flood, drought, plague) than nomadic groups. It also makes it more difficult to flee invaders, because there is a certain area that must be protected for the survival of the group.

However, a properly-tended agricultural settlement can yield much greater results than an equivalent nomadic group would. This creates a large food surplus, which is a necessity for creating specialized jobs and professions other than "farmer". While most agricultural societies throughout history were composed *mostly* of farmers (70% to 90%), the non-farmer sections of society could specialize in tasks such as mining, building, crafting, and so on. This sort of specialization was necessary for the development of technology and organized institutions.

Survival for any society, nomadic or sedentary, is predicated on their ability to turn natural phenomena such as plants or animals to their ongoing advantage. Hunter-gatherer peoples learn the patterns of nature, what is advantageous to them and what is harmful. They may even engage in shaping the world around them with low-intensity gardens or selective planting. But a more complex society needs a more reliable supply of resources, and for this reason the taming of nature, or at least its coercion, is necessary.

<u>Horticulture</u> is the act of raising, nourishing and harvesting beneficial plants and fungi. Plants are generally grown for four main reasons: for food, for manufacturing & crafting, for medicine, and for anesthetics. As with animals, many plants fit into multiple uses (often by using different parts of the plant).

Horticulture requires fertile land with a reliable water source. The earliest sedentary societies formed around rivers such as the Euphrates, Tigris, Indus and Nile. Land fertility is related to the composition of the soil. Natural fertilizers can be carried by wind (*loess*) or water (*silt*). Creating fertile land, or maintaining it after farming, is a complicated, multi-layered process that involves ensuring the proper balance of materials found in the soil. A naturally created "fertile area" may have been shaped over the course of millions of years of soil movement. Conversely, a fertile area can be easily depleted by removing enough plants without replacing them, or planting in a way that saps nutrients from the soil. For this reason, many cultures developed *crop rotation*, which seasonally exchanges plants in order to ensure the proper balance of chemicals being added to, and depleted from, the earth.

An alternative to crop rotation is *companion planting*, in which crops are grown together in order to benefit each other during their development. Many **Native American** peoples, including the **Haudenosaunee**, used a system they called "three sisters". This consisted of maize, winter squash, and climbing beans. The bean plants climb the maize stalks, and provide nitrogen to the soil. The squash is used to secure the lower levels by blocking sunlight with its broad leaves. This does not affect the beans or maize (both of which are higher than the squash) but prevents ground-level weeds from growing. The squash leaves also support moisture retaining in the soil. Another example comes from **China**, where rice plants are partnered with *azolla*, which acts as fertilizer and also blocks competing plants at ground level.

A *staple crop* is a food crop that forms the largest, most reliable part of a culture's harvest. While most societies grew as many useful plants as they could, certain crops formed the foundation of their diet, and were grown in majority numbers. Some examples of staple crops include *wheat, rice, maize* and *potatoes*. While most regions had a single staple crop, with the advent of trade this limit was no longer necessary. More specific regional staple foods include *yams* (sub-Saharan Africa), *taro* (southeast Asia), *cassava* (South America) and *soybeans* (east Asia). A staple crop forms the base of a culture's culinary designs, being the most efficient and hardy plant in a given culture's repertoire. However, most cultures attempt to avoid overspecialization, because diseases and blights tend to spread by type. The Great Famine in **Ireland** was caused by English colonial policies, which forced natives to subsist on cheap, easily grown potatoes instead of the broader range of plants. When potatoes were infected with a blight, the people of Ireland lost one of their primary food sources and starved.

An *industrial crop* is a non-food crop that is harvested for use in crafting or mixing. Plants grown for purposes of crafting clothing or rope are called *fiber crops*, which are a form of plant textile (as opposed to animal textiles such as hair). Plant textiles include *flax* (which becomes linen), *cotton, bamboo, hemp, straw, grass* and *jute*. Medicinal herbs also fall under the "industrial crops" category, as do plants used for oils, inks and dyes.

Farming often requires landscaping or earth-moving in order to create a flat environment that can be properly tilled for sowing seeds. In hilly or mountainous regions, this has led to *terraced farming*, where the landscape is flattened into periodic "steps" to create multiple layers of flat ground. The steps are sometimes held in place with stone or wood walls. Terraced farming has been historically practiced across the world, perhaps most famously by the **Inca** people. However, almost any mountainous region may have some history of it, including **Scotland**, **Tibet**, **Nepal**, the **Canary Islands**, and throughout southeast Asia.

Another construction usually required for farming is *irrigation*. Irrigation means transferring water to the desired farming area, either by means of digging down to groundwater under the earth (creating a *well*) or diverting water from rivers, lakes and aquifers with *canals* or *aqueducts*. These methods are also used to provide population centers with water for drinking or cleaning purposes. Some examples of historical irrigation projects include the **Iranian** *qanat* tunnels, the Eupalinian Aqueduct of **Samos**, and the **Peruvian** *Puquios*. Some crops do not require irrigation, either because the plants themselves do not require much water (winter wheat, maize, beans) or because the plants are capable of using stored moisture in the soil (grapes, tomatoes, pumpkins). These are called *dryland farming* and *dry farming* respectively.

Land in a sedentary society could either be owned by individuals or families, or it could be held in common. In **Greece** and **Rome**, for example, land was bought and passed down through families. Rich landowners crowding out the livelihood of poorer farmers was a frequent problem. In other places, land was held in common by a village or similar small unit, although the village itself might be under the jurisdiction of a lord. The *open field system* in **Europe** was an example of this, and was used for the majority of lands in medieval times. In **Russia**, the *obshchina* system was similar, where tracts of land would be parceled out among a village's population in order to make sure all members were productive - and thus capable of paying taxes.

Many places would use a combination of owned land and common land. For example, in **Japan**, the forested areas at the foothills of mountains and hills (*satoyama*) were accepted as common areas where any farmer could gather leaves, kindling and wood for building. In **England**, after the open field system was revoked, certain areas remained for common usage - not for planting, but for things such as pasturing animals, fishing, extracting surface resources such as turf or clay, or taking wood. Eventually even this common land was also partially privatized, and the majority of land was owned privately under the system of *enclosure*.

In **China's** Zhou period, the *"well-field system"* consisted of a 3x3 grid of land parcels. All nine parcels were technically owned by an aristocrat, but the outer eight would each be managed by individual peasant families, and the materials produced would be their own. The central square would be worked by all eight peasant families, and all materials produced there would be taken by the owning aristocrat as his share. This system would be eventually replaced by other systems, such as wholly private ownership. The *tuntian* system, developed by Chancellor Cao Cao of the Han dynasty, involved land and farming equipment being given cheaply to landless farmers or retired soldiers. In return for this initial investment, the farmer owned half of his crop to the noble who owned it. This provided many displaced refugees with a place to live and a way to provide for themselves, and also provided the noble with plenty of materials to supply his armies.

Domestication is the act of turning a wild animal into a reliably subservient animal, through the act of training, coercion and selective breeding (*husbandry*). Domestication is an important tool in human history because it allowed humans to create beneficial relationships and turn less useful resources (such as grass) into more useful ones. There are essentially three roles of domestication, and domesticated animals may overlap with multiple roles. These roles are *resources*, *work*, and *pets*.

Resource animals are valued for the materials they produce. A cow, for example, produces milk, hair and dung (fertilizer) while it lives, and meat and leather if it is killed. Other common animals that fall under this category include pigs, chickens, sheep, goats, reindeer, llamas, rabbits, silkworms and bees.

Work animals are valued for the labor they contribute. Horses, for example, can be ridden, or they can be yoked to ploughs or wagons. On the other end of the scale, cats were useful to humans throughout history because they exterminate rodents that threaten crop supplies. Dogs provide protection and can be trained to assist in hunting or herding. Other work animals include donkeys, camels, ferrets, and pigeons.

Pets are not expected to fulfill any particular utilitarian role, but exist because their owners find them endearing or comforting. In modern times, many animals that once served a utilitarian purpose are still kept around as pets. In ancient **Greece**, apes and monkeys were commonly kept as pets, as well as snakes, ducks and geese. The **Orang Asli** people of modern Malaysia domesticated a local civet called the *binturong* as a pet.

Many animals fall under multiple roles; cattle, for example, are used both for resources and for plowing fields, pulling carts, etc. Horses are primarily a work animal, but in horse-specialized societies, they are also used for milk and meat. Dogs and cats are work animals but also pets, and (in some parts of the world) also used for meat. Societies may have taboos against eating certain animals based on attachment and relationships; most views of cats and dogs are an example of this, but so is the Hindu relationship with cattle. Cattle are seen as kind and giving, since they provide so many resources and services to humans; the act of killing them to take *more* resources is considered barbaric.

In terms of diversity, there are some core "archetypes" of domestic animal that can be modified region-by-region. The role of a large, milk-giving heavy ungulate is commonly taken by cattle, but can also describe yaks, bison, zebu, water buffalo, and so on. When designing a culture, it might benefit you to determine the region they will be living in and then map out the appropriate animal types from there.

Similarly, the *lack* of a certain animal type might play a large role in one's culture. The Americas lacked both horses and domesticated cattle until European settlers arrived. **South American** peoples had llamas and alpacas for wool and light burden-bearing, but that was essentially it. There were no animals for practical riding or heavy labor. The introduction of horses especially was a major change for **North American Plains Peoples**, and they adapted quickly into "horse cultures".

6.2 Crafting & Materials

A culture's ability to craft is connected both to their available resources and their available technology. An abundance of iron is useless if you don't know how to work it, and knowing how to work iron isn't particularly helpful if it's rare. "Crafting" as a broad term is responsible for everything from clothing to tools to decoration, and understanding *how* those things are made is a vital part of creating a culture.

Handicrafts are the most "base" level of crafting. The term refers to any craft made with only one's hands, or with simple handheld tools. In some cases, handicrafting involves using resources that are easily available in nature, such as wood, bone, stone, shells, straw, grass, reeds, rushes, animal sinews, and so on. Others require more complex structures to either complete the process (clay into ceramics) or to provide the initial workable material in the first place (knitting requires yarn, cobbling requires leather, etc.). Handicrafting exists at some level no matter how industrialized or developed a given culture gets; it's mostly just a question of *which* crafts are made more easily through industrial means.

Some examples of basic handicrafts made without other complex items include:
- basket-weaving (grasses/rushes, wicker, broad leaves)
- stone-chipping (a hard stone & a "tool stone" like flint)
- wood-carving (wood & sharpened stone)
- tool-making (wood, stone & fibers or sinew)
- jewelry (precious material & fibers or sinew)

A kiln is an oven designed to heat clay into ceramics, smelting ore to extract metal, and drying certain plants or materials. They traditionally consist of a raised platform surrounded by earth or bricks, with a fireplace underneath and a hole for smoke in the top. However, there are many different types, suited for different purposes. Kilns can be considered in some ways to be the first step towards greater industry, since they can be made out of non-crafted materials (earth and wood) and they enable the creation of items that themselves allow further development.

Ceramics are clay shaped into useful items, such as plates, bowls or pots, and then hardened with heat. Bricks are made in a similar way, although their composition is slightly different. Bricks were often made in large mold-trays, which would be heated all at once. These are specifically known as *fired* bricks, which differentiates them from the older method of sun-drying bricks (the former are more durable than the latter).Ceramic roof tiles such as those found in **Greece** or **Rome** are also produced in kilns.

Smelting is the process of heating rocks containing metallic elements, in conjunction with an agent called a *reducer*. The goal is to break and decompose the rock parts, leaving only liquid metal behind. The liquid metal is then poured (or streamed) into a casting basin, where it cools and forms an *ingot*. The ingot is then transportable for use in later shaping. Of note: some metals (such as gold, silver and copper) can be found "as metals" without the need for smelting. In this form, they are referred to as *native metals* (i.e. native copper). Native metals are likely the source for the earliest smithing, or at least metal-crafting. Iron could also be found as a native, in the form of meteoric iron.

Finally, *drying* is the act of heating a plant to induce a chemical change. One of the most common examples of kiln-drying is the creation of charcoal. Essentially, a large amount of wood was intentionally burned up (which would take several days, and had to be watched continuously to prevent the fire from going out of control). A common classical charcoal kiln consisted of a pile of firewood covered with earth, with a hole at the top for oxygen and smoke to flow. Charcoal is valuable as a fuel for most forms of smithing since it burns incredibly hot, but is especially valuable in steel-making because of the carbons it contributes to the process.

A <u>forge</u> is an oven, often open-faced, used to heat metal for purposes of shaping. The heated metal is pounded into place with a hammer, either delicately (by the smith himself, with a small hammer) or more forcefully (by an assistant wielding a larger hammer). The hammering is done on an anvil, a heavy metal item used as a hard surface, but which also has other roles in shaping heated metal. Heated items would be quenched in water or oils, either to cool them for inspection or to introduce certain chemical properties (*quench-hardening*). Tongs were used to transport the heated item from forge to anvil to quenching-pool.

The end goal of forging an item is that when the metal finally cools, it will have sufficient hardness and structure to be used for tools, weapons, or other purposes. Notably, the smith's role in toolmaking means that a smith is necessary for the improved performance of many other parts of society, including farmers, miners, and other craftsmen. The act of smithing is laborious and requires constant maintenance, and the secrets of proper temperature were regarded as near-magic in ancient times.

The earliest smithing was done with native metals (described above). When smelting became more well-known, tools were made out of copper, and then out of bronze (which is mostly copper, with some tin). Iron became prominent with the **Hittites** in the 1500s BCE, although it was softer than bronze. However, compared to bronze, iron had an advantage of simplicity: ironworking required only one metal, whereas bronze required two. It was possible to deprive a bronze-using civilization of their supply of either tin or copper and essentially destroy their metal economy in that manner.

The difference became even more severe with the discovery of steel, which *was* stronger than bronze, and required only iron along with some carbonizing elements.

A loom is a wooden device used to turn fibers into fabric. Fibers (such as linen, cotton, wool, silk) are first spun together to form thread. This process can be done by hand (with the aid of simple tools such as a *spinning jug*) or it can be done on a wooden *spinning jenny*. Once the thread is spun, the loom layers it by stringing a piece of thread (the *weft*) through other parallel-layered pieces (the *warp*), using a guide called a *shuttle,* in order to create a solid piece of fabric. Looms can be small and portable, in the form of *back strap looms*, although even these must be tied to somewhere high up in order to give them the necessary elevation.

The larger, more complex *warp-weighted loom* has a history that is just as old as the back strap loom; the earliest found comes from the Neolithic period. Warp-weighted looms consist of two tall pieces of wood with a thick upper crossbar at their top and a thinner lower crossbar in their middle. The threads are strung between the upper and middle crossbars, and are kept taut with heavy weights tied to the lower strands.

Beyond this, there are two larger and more complex types of loom - the *drawloom* and *handloom* that take up much more space and are far more involved in terms of their construction. However, their materials are still relatively simple (i.e. "mostly wood"). Discovering the technology and systems necessary was more troublesome than finding the necessary materials. These sorts of looms were also limited to sedentary cultures, whereas backstrap looms and warp-weighted looms were more portable.

Tanneries are sites where animal hides are treated to be turned into leather. It is a noxious and pungent task, so much so that tanning sites throughout the world are kept far away from other inhabited areas. In many cases it was performed by an "untouchable" caste, who were considered the only ones low-rank enough to perform such a task. Nevertheless, tanning produces a valuable resource, which can be used for clothing, holding items, or animal harnesses/saddles. It can also be cut into strips, which can be used in a way similar to fibrous rope.

Tanning begins with animal skins, which are, naturally, cut off of the animal. The skin is first cleaned in water, then scrubbed of any flesh or fat to ensure purity. Next, hair/fur was loosened by one of several methods, including dipping the skin in urine. Once loosened the hair/fur would be removed with a knife or other sharp implement. Next, the skin would be softened by being soaked in water mixed with either dung or animal brains. Finally, the skin is exposed to tannin, an acidic substance taken from certain plants and tree bark.

Lacquer is a resin-derived material that gives items a glossy, solid-looking finish. Usually, lacquered items are originally made of wood, leather, or metal. Lacquer can be taken from tree sap (specifically the Chinese Lacquer Tree, or the Thitsi tree of southeast Asia) or from Lac insects. The resin is mixed with pigments and stirred until it has lost its water content, at which point it is applied to the material. In addition to aesthetic purposes, lacquering also helps with water-proofing and preservation. **Japanese** armor (leather or metal) was often lacquered for utility purposes, which also allowed it to carry bright, distinct colors. Lacquerware in general is common across east Asia, including **China**, **India**, **Vietnam**, **Thailand**, **Burma** and the **Ryukyu Islands**.

Mills are complex machines that use gears attached to a driving power to achieve various effects. *Watermills* are built next to rivers or other flowing water, and use a large wheel to generate momentum from the flow. *Windmills* are erected in open areas and have large sails that catch the wind to turn the mechanisms. *Animal-driven mills* use circular walking motions of a work animal as their power source. Mill mechanisms can be used for a variety of purposes that require repetitive but powerful movements, such as separating grain, stamping ore, sawing logs, pumping bellows, and so on. Most mill mechanisms originated in **Greece** or **China** and spread outwards from there; during China's *Han* dynasty, the astronomer Zhang Heng even built a water-powered spherical astrolabe for purposes of mapping the stars.

Another use of mill-like machines is drawing up water into a reservoir or aqueduct. These machines use repetitive movements like a mill, but their end effect is drawing water up from under the earth into a reservoir or aqueduct. Examples of these machines include the *noria*, which uses water, the *sakia*, which uses animals, and the *windpump*, which uses wind. The noria model originated in **Greece**, spread to **Rome**, and from there was used most commonly in the **Arab** world. The windpump, on the other hand, came from 9th century south-central

Asia (**Afghanistan**, **Pakistan**, and eastern **Iran**) and spread to the Arab world as well as **China** and **India**.

6.3 Buildings & Architecture

Shelter is a necessity of human existence. While nomadic peoples or hunter-gatherers create relatively simple camps of animal skin tents, a sedentary society has more complex needs. Their stationary nature means that they can invest in much more stable and protective structures, but they also require fortifications to protect those structures from attack. The buildings created by a given culture depend on both their need and their available resources. The first step, therefore, is discussing building materials.

Timbers are large, cut pieces of solid wood used to act as a framework for greater constructions. Timber is rarely used as a "building material" on its own, but rather is used to support walls made from the other described materials. They are not the oldest construction type, but they are described first here because they provide framework for many other types of material construction.

Rammed earth is a building style popular across the world, from **China** (*hangtu*) to **Wales** (*cob*) to **Morocco** (*pisé*). The earliest recorded usage is by soldiers of **Carthage**, but the oldest sites date back to 5000 BCE in China. Rammed earth construction involves setting up a wooden frame or mold, similar to concrete. The two halves of the mold are clamped in place to maintain equal distance and prevent bulging or weaknesses. The mold is then filled with damp earth, which is compacted with a ramming pole. Once it is suitably packed in, the molds are removed and the earth is allowed to dry. During this period, the walls are sometimes patterned or engraved, in a manner similar to writing in wet cement.

Thatch is a building material made of dried vegetation; in most cases, thatch is used for roofing purposes. Grasses or rushes are most commonly identified as "thatch" materials and are used everywhere from **England** to **India** to **Japan**. However, other plant-based construction methods exist and these are also referred to as thatch. One example is palm leaves, used in tropical regions such as the **Caribbean, Central America** or **Southeast Asia**. Sometimes thatch is used for the entire building frame, such as in **Sub-Saharan Africa**, among the **Marsh Arab** peoples, among the **Ainu** of northern Japan, or among the **Inca**, **Maya**, and **Aztec**.

Animal skins are propped up on wooden poles to form tents. These can be the *teepees* of the **American Plains** peoples, the *yurts* of the **Turkic** peoples, or the *gers* of the **Mongolians**. The first written description of such a dwelling comes from Herodotus, who describes the Eastern European **Scythians** living in such dwellings. Such dwellings are lightweight, which suits the nomadic lifestyle. The Plains peoples would sometimes supplement the animal skins with straw, which was stuffed between the interior and exterior layers, during cold weather.

Wattle & daub construction consists of two parts: woven lattices made of thin wood (the *wattle*) and a sticky composite made of soil, clay, dung and straw (*daub*). The result is a hardened material attached to a wooden framework, which grants solid insulation properties. Wattle and daub buildings can be found in prehistoric **Germany & Turkey**, amongst the **Mississippian Cultures**, with the **Ashanti** peoples of Ghana, in Iron Age **Britain**, and in many other parts of the world. Wattle & daub provides the framework for the oldest form of timber-framed construction.

Brick is made by loading earth and clay into a frame, which produces many small blocks that can be assembled after drying. Individual bricks are fused together with *mortar*, which is made out of resin, bitumen and clay. There are two kinds of brick: *sun-dried* bricks, which are weaker and require a binding element such as straw, and *kiln-fired* bricks, which are stronger and more permanent. Sun-dried bricks were an integral component of many early cities, such as *Mohenjo-Daro* of the **Indus Valley Civilization**, **Minoan** *Knossos*, and the **Mesopotamian** cities of *Sumer*, *Ur*, *Akkad*, and *Babylon*. They were also used by the **Pueblo** people of the American Southwest, and by the people of the sub-Saharan **Sahel** region. Kiln-fired bricks were first used in the Indus Valley, then later in **China** and **Greece**. They were spread across Europe by the **Romans**, whose legions would produce brick buildings as they conquered and resettled areas. Ceramic *tiles* were made of clay in a manner similar to fired brick; these were used for housing by the Chinese, Greeks, and Romans - the latter culture ensuring their spread amongst the other peoples of Europe. Tiles were heavier than material such as thatch, and required a strong support structure to hold up. However, they were more fire-resistant than thatch, which was beneficial in enclosed cities.

Log construction originated in Scandinavia amongst the **Nordic** peoples and the **Finns,** with findings dating back to the Bronze Age. The first referenced description of log structures dates back to Iron Age **Pontus**, on the southeast coast of the Black Sea. According to the Roman architect Vitruvius, these early log houses were made by overlapping logs to form walls, with indentations made at the overlaps to facilitate interlocking. The gaps between the logs were filled with chips and mud. Log construction is heavily dependent on an availability of tall, solid trees, and such trees are easily found in Scandinavia and Russia. A benefit of certain styles, such as the **Russian** *izba*, is that nails are not necessary - a blessing in iron-poor regions.

Planks are used to fill in timber frames in the same way that wattle & daub or bricks are. A plank is a flat-cut section of wood that varies in size. In post-and-plank construction, planks were cut large enough to fill the gap between timber frames. This construction technique dates back to the Bronze Age with the **Lusatian** culture in central Europe. The similar wooden shingle was used for roofing in northern and eastern Europe. A less common form of plank structure was the *plank house* developed by the **Northwest American Indigenous Peoples**, including the **Coast Salish**, **Yurok** and **Chinook**. These buildings were built of cedar planks, with cedar logs forming the core framing. The planks were not cut from fallen trees but were harvested from living trees through a long process of wedging and cutting. The planks were held in place by ropes lashing together multiple parts of the frame; the pressure from the ropes held the lighter planks in place. Due to this form of construction, these houses could be disassembled and brought from place to place if necessary.

Stone construction involves either collecting rocks or shaping solid stone into blocks (small-to-medium) or slabs (large). These components are assembled into walls, which are sometimes used on their own and sometimes used as foundations or support for other types of construction (such as earthworks). Some stone structures stand on their own, using gravity and compression to hold the work together. This is called *dry stone* or *drystack*. Other structures, typically larger ones, require mortar to maintain cohesion, in a way similar to brick. Because of the solidity and permanence of the building materials, stone structures provide relatively solid artifacts of ancient culture. These include the cities of the **Inca** and **Aztecs** in America, of the **Egyptians**, **Shona** and **baKoni** in Africa, of the **Khmer** and **Rakhine** in Asia, of the **Celts** and **Greeks** in Europe, and so on.

Plaster is not a building material on its own, but rather a layer applied to other forms of building such as brick, planks or wattle & daub. Plaster consists of a dry powder made of gypsum or lime, which is mixed with water to form a sort of paste. The paste is applied to a wall, where it quickly hardens to form an additional solid layer. Plaster often serves a cosmetic purpose, as it can be inscribed or painted relatively easily. It also serves a practical purpose, in that it is relatively weather-resistant and can protect more vulnerable core materials beneath it. The oldest plaster usage was found in **Jordan**, **India**, **China** and **Egypt**, and these examples were often painted over or otherwise decorated.

Once the available materials are established, then the question of <u>urban planning</u> becomes important. Most sedentary cultures consisted of a series of *villages*, which served as a hub for farmsteads, lumber camps, mines, and other resource gathering sites. Villages tended to be simple in nature, providing services & supplies to the small outlying community. For example, a village might have a church or temple, a smith for tools, a tavern, and so on. Above those were *towns*, which had a higher population of craftsmen and traders to process and disseminate the resources gathered in rural areas. *Cities* are the largest category, and these in turn act as a larger hub to towns. Because of the complex nature of towns and cities, the act of making room and supplying services for inhabitants become more intense.

Some of the first cities known in history are the ones from the **Harappan** civilization. Harappan cities were remarkably complex, especially given their age. Cities were built of brick structures arranged on pre-designed grids. Public baths, marketplaces, and wells served as hubs within the city, and examples of indoor plumbing (complete with underground sewage drainage and hydraulic water systems) were common.

Many other early civilizations practiced urban planning, including the **Mesopotamian** cultures. In "The Epic of Gilgamesh", this dialogue occurs: *"Gilgamesh said to Urshanabi, the ferryman: "Go up, Urshanabi, onto the wall of Uruk and walk around. Examine its foundation, inspect its brickwork thoroughly—is not (even the core of) the brick structure of kiln-fired brick, and did not the Seven Sages themselves lay out its plan? One league city, one league palm gardens, one league lowlands, the open area(?) of the Ishtar Temple, three leagues and the open area(?) of Uruk it (the wall) encloses.""* These careful measurements, and the boasting of their precision, gives insight into the care with which cities of this early era were built.

Despite this early evidence, the **Greek** cultures believed that Hippodamus of Miletus was "the father of urban planning", giving his name to a grid system known as the *Hippodamian Plan*. His designs involved a broad grid of streets built around a wide central area, or *agora*, which could be used as a marketplace, assembly area, and so on. Another famous Greek urban planner was Dinocrates, who designed the city of Alexandria in Egypt. Alexandria, at the time, was considered the world's greatest example of city design, and contained hydraulic water systems and pumps (partly by necessity due to the city's water level).

The **Romans** built off the Hippodamian model, with grid streets based around a central *forum*. The Romans developed the *insulae*, which were large structures used for shops (lower floor) and apartments (upper floors). Through the use of these structures, the Romans were able to provide housing for a great number of low-income workers. Lower floors were considered more desirable than upper floors, as they were safer, better heated, and had easier access to running water or drainage systems. The Romans also commonly provided public baths (*balneae*) and public toilets (*latrinae*), which helped to fight disease.

In **China**, the peoples of the *Zhou* dynasty used a complex system of spiritual principles to justify its urban planning. They used a concept called a *holy field*, which was a square pattern based on numerological beliefs originating from the *Shang* period. The end result was a 3x3 pattern with different building types (such as temples, shrines, and markets) assigned to different parts of the square based on their symbology. The pattern's overall layout depended on the size of the city, but the core square layout was preferred regardless of size. Even within the cities, individual blocks would be planned out in a pattern called a *siheyuan*. This was essentially a walled, gated compound containing several sub-buildings arranged around a central courtyard. The siheyuan pattern was used from everything to residential to monastic to bureaucratic purposes. Chinese design patterns were first codified in the *Rites of Zhou*, a general guidebook for governance and administration.

An alternative Chinese model was used by the **Hakka** people of southern China. They used donut-shaped apartment buildings called *tulou*. Tulou were designed to be defensible, and were made of earth, stone, and brick. At their center was a shrine. In addition to residential quarters, each tulou also contained a well, an armory and grain storage for the event of an attack. In essence, the tulou was a fortress-apartment. Another alternative was the *yaodong*, found in China's northern Huangtu Plateau. A Yaodong was a home partially built into a cave wall. The exterior is shored up with bricks or stone, while the interior is cut into the cave wall itself. The building method creates good natural insulation, although historically such homes are vulnerable to earthquakes and similar seismic activity.

The **Celts** used a town model that the Romans called an "*oppidum*", or "enclosed space". Oppida were not uniform, and were used contemporarily to describe a variety of towns and cities. However, there were some common threads. The walls of an oppida were usually earthworks faced with a stone base and wooden palisades. Most were built on high, defensible areas with a wide view of the region. Within an oppida were contained crafting areas, smithies, religious sites, burial grounds, and small farming areas for nobility. The oppida of *Bibracte* had heating and sewer systems made of wood, inspired heavily by Roman influences. Most homes in Bibracte were made of earth and wood, with stone being saved for the noble houses and the walls.

The **Teotihuacanos** of Mexico predated both the Aztecs and the Spanish invasion. Their city of Teotihuacan was established around 100 BCE, and was built up until its destruction around 500 CE. In that time period it was the most populated site in the region and exerted the most influence. The city was home to many craftsmen - obsidian-workers, jewelers, mural-artists, and so on. Many temples and religious sites were step pyramids built in the *talud-tablero* style. The city was also home to many apartment buildings, which were inhabited by most citizens regardless of social class.

A sedentary village, town or city is an obvious target for raiders or invaders. Unlike a nomadic settlement, a sedentary settlement cannot be easily moved, and thus the community cannot "evade" an enemy attack. Instead, it must prepare for it and try to hold it off. This is where fortification comes from.

Fortifications are commonly made of wood (*palisade*) or stone. An example of an ancient fortified site is Solnitsata, a **Bulgarian** settlement from 4700 BCE that was surrounded by 10-foot-tall stone walls. Solnitsata was a salt mine, and salt was incredibly valuable as a food preservative - which explains the measures taken to protect the site. In **Mesopotamia**, mud bricks were common for fortification, and mud-brick walls provide some of the earliest examples of city walls (such as those around Uruk). In **China**, walls were built primarily with rammed earth until the 5th century BCE, when stone walls began to be used.

In addition to walls, high ground was also utilized for tactical advantages. For example, the *motte-and-bailey* castle used by the **Normans** (among others) consisted of an enclosed lower section (the bailey) and a central keep located on a raised mound or hill (the motte). The *hill forts* used by the **Celts** and other societies across Europe were built entirely on hilltops to take advantage of the terrain. The **Maori** had a similar kind of fortification - a complex of palisades and towers called a *pā*.

Fortifications were also supplemented with ditches outside their walls, sometimes filled with sharpened stakes or water (a *moat*). Construction would often include features to make combat more advantageous for the defender, such as *arrow slits* that protected archers while allowing them to fire out. In the case of more advanced fortifications, the defender's advantage was so formidable that attackers would simply surround the town and deny it food or supplies, rather than actually attempting to take the walls by force.

Walled complexes - whether towns, forts or castles - conveyed a certain amount of power and independence among its inhabitants. Charles the Bald of **West Francia** prohibited the unauthorized construction of fortifications (*castella*) by his subordinates, and ordered any such fortification to be torn down. After the collapse of the Frankish empire, individual lords and nobles began to project their power from their own fortified homes. This was the beginning of the feudal castle system in **Europe**.

6.4 Trade & Communication

One of the oldest problems facing humans is overabundance of some materials, and underabundance of others. This could be done on a personal level (a shepherd needs things besides wool and sheep's milk) or on a societal level (a fertile region might have low metal content). As such, people began to trade, exchanging their overabundant material for someone else's overabundant material. This kind of trade is called barter - an item for an item.

However, this required what is called a *"coincidence of wants"*, which is to say it is only possible to trade an item that (a) you have, and (b) the other person wants, regardless of what it is you're trading for. Another problem is that certain types of item are seasonal, such as crops, and trading them in the present is not always possible.

Due to the imperfections of the barter system, commodity money (also known as *"proto-money"*) was developed. These were items perceived to have intrinsic value that were easily transportable and transferable. A unit of commodity money would have value no matter what it was traded for, although the value of the item itself would depend on supply and demand.

During **China**'s *Shang* dynasty (18th-12th century BCE), cowry shells were used as currency, and eventually imitation shells made of metal were used as currency as well. Later, small bronze spades were used instead. The **Celts** made small items of bronze for trading, including bells, axeheads, and rings. They would also make lesser currencies out of "potin", which was similar to bronze but had a higher tin composition (the Romans also used it for low-denomination coinage). In **West Africa**, a metal semicircle called a *manilla* was used, and its use continues in some areas even to the present day. The **Polish** *grzywna* was a standardized-size silver ingot with a hole punched in the top, that could be easily carried around on a loop of rope or leather.

Another alternative to such items was a valuable, universally-useful material resource. In **Canada**, for example, fur traders had constant need of beaver pelts. Thus, the beaver pelt became a form of commodity money, since native peoples could trade beaver pelts for whatever they needed (tools, clothes, weapons, etc.). In ancient **Sumer**, the *shekel* was developed - a weight of barley used as a common trade good. Compared to metal items, such commodity monies had disadvantages in terms of their durability and permanence.

The advent of coinage allowed for a relatively lightweight, standardized form of currency. Coins had both intrinsic value (being composed of precious metals) and state-supported value. Unlike commodity monies, coins were made by governments, not simply found. Their weight and composition were controlled by the governments that commissioned them, and stamped with images relevant to them. Coins were also small, allowing them to be carried around more easily than the sometimes-awkward shapes of commodity monies.

Coins were made by creating a mold with many small circular indentations in them. Molten metal was poured into these indentations to form the base coin, or "blank". These blanks were then placed on a coining anvil, and they were struck with a *die*, or metal stamp. The resulting impact would produce two imprints on the metal: one from the anvil, and the other from the stamp. This would produce a double-sided coin.

The first coins in history were produced in **Aegina** (a Greek island) and **Lydia** (now western Turkey) in the 7th century BCE. **India** followed about a century thereafter, and **China** another century after that (although it is arguable they may have produced the oldest example). Chinese coins were made with a hole in the center, so that they could be strung together in a manner similar to the Polish grzywna.

Once banks became strong enough, money could be made in such a way that it contained no intrinsic value of its own, but rather was dependent entirely on the presumed value it represented. These were promissory notes, and they essentially operated on trust value. If a government collapses, a gold coin still contains gold, which is inherently valuable to most cultures. However, a promissory note, made of paper (*bank notes*) or wood (*tally sticks*), was reliant entirely on the support and trust of the issuing institution. Tally sticks were common as a memory device throughout history, even before civilization. The **English** crown turned them into a form of money in the 12th century AD. Paper money, on the other hand, was developed in **China** - first under the Tang dynasty, and more fully under the Song. When the **Mongols** took control of China (as the Yuan dynasty), they expanded the role of paper money. This eventually caught the attention of Marco Polo, who brought the idea back to **Italy**. Despite their vulnerabilities, these forms of currency were far more transportable than precious metals were, and thus fulfilled an important role in large-scale trading.

An important tool for trading was record-keeping. The first writing in history was done in **Mesopotamia** in approximately 8000 BCE. This early writing was in the form of pictograms carved into *clay tablets*, and their purpose was recording trades or debts. As such, the first pictograms that were developed were based on trade-goods. These pictograms were rendered in shorthand and abstracted more and more, forming a vaguer, but more complex, system of writing. Eventually, they were used to represent syllables of speech, at which point they were able to transcribe stories, information and events in a more complex manner. Writing in one form or another spread throughout the world, but that was no guarantee that the majority of people would be *literate*. In many cases, knowledge of writing was kept only to the upper classes or the priesthood. Other early adopters of writing include **China** (6500 BCE, developed independently) **Egypt** (4000 BCE, based on Mesopotamia), and **Mexico** (1000 BCE, developed independently). Apart from clay tablets, writing was also done on bone, shell, bamboo, stone, metal and wood. In **Greece**, shards of pottery were essentially used as "scrap paper" because they were commonly available, unlike other materials which were more expensive.

Eventually, lighter-weight materials were introduced, which required more processing to create but also made transportation and storage easier. One such material was *papyrus*, which was made of reeds woven and possibly glued together by the ancient Egyptians. Papyrus was useful in dry climates, but developed mold eventually in wetter climes, reducing their lifespan to a few decades before degrading. However, they are still commonly used in wet regions, such as warm swamps, because the plants they come from grow commonly in those regions.

Another alternative was *parchment*, which was made of cleaned-and-dried animal skins. Parchment originated in the region of **Anatolia** (modern day Turkey) and was mentioned as being in common use by the Greek historian Herodotus. One early justification for the usage of parchment was that the region of **Pergamon** was unable to obtain papyrus and was forced to find an alternative. Parchment responds poorly to changes in humidity, which is why bound books of parchment from the Renaissance often have metal clasps to hold them shut. The purpose is not to "lock" the book so much as it is to hold the book together, thus keeping the pages flat.

Finally, we come to *paper*. Paper was invented in China shortly before the BCE-CE transition. It was made from tree bark and fibrous rags combined in water. The solid material was crushed and beaten to form a liquid mixture, and then modifier chemicals were added. The mixture was then poured out onto a fabric cloth and allowed to dry. This created a lightweight writing material that was less temperamental than papyrus or parchment. The Chinese originally held onto the secret for many centuries, but it was eventually spread out to the Islamic world and from there to Europe.

In regions without writing, or amongst illiterate peoples, information was maintained through *oral tradition*. In essence, a story would be remembered by a designated individual, who would pass it down to another when the time was right, on and on throughout history. The weakness of oral tradition is that memorization is a long and difficult process, especially for more complex stories. The foibles of memory also render it as an imperfect information storage vehicle, which would be compounded over generations as each new teller would get it somehow wrong and carry those errors to the next teller.

There were other forms of more immediate communication. In **West Africa**, *drums* carried information across densely forested regions that were otherwise difficult to traverse. The beats and patterns could convey information, and some drums (*talking drums*) were shaped to make sounds similar to human speech.

Smoke signals were also used in several regions to convey messages across long, open distances. This was accomplished by lighting a fire and then interrupting it periodically with a blanket or other suppressant. The first un-patterned version of this was used on the Great Wall of **China**, then later in **Greece** in its more complex form. It was developed independently by the aboriginal peoples of **North America** and **Australia**, as well as the **Yaghan** peoples of the archipelagic tip of South America.

Beacon chains consisted of a relay of stations, each within visual range of the former and next. A torch or light created at one station would be noticed by the next station, which would then light its own beacon, which would be noticed by the next, and so on and so forth. Such beacons were common throughout ancient Europe; in many places, such as **Wales**, **Finland** and **Scotland**, they existed to warn of incoming raids. Arguably the most complex beacon chain was the **Byzantine** beacon system, which stretched from Constantinople out to the border at Cicilia. This was a 450-mile journey, and stations were placed anywhere from 35 to 60 miles apart. Messages could be sent from one end of the system to the other in about an hour.

A device called a *hydraulic semaphore* was used in the ancient world for long-distance communication. The historian Polybius describes it as being used to send information from **Sicily** to **Carthage**. The device itself consisted of sets of identical water containers containing a vertical rod inscribed with various codes. Its usage was somewhat complex; one station would signal another by lighting a torch. When the other had lit their own torch in return, the two would synchronize, and then drain their containers at the same time. Once the desired level was reached, the transmitting operator would lower their torch, and the receiver would reseal the container. The water level would correspond to a section of the vertical rod, and this would convey the necessary information. Polybius describes this as a troublesome method of communication, or at least one that "fell short of our requirements".

Finally, in addition to these forms of communication, direct movement - or travel - was also a massive influence on both trade and cultural contact. Whether by land or sea, different cultures would find ways to reach new regions, meet new peoples, and acquire new resources.

Basic water travel involved either a river or, in an open body of water, staying close to shore to maintain visual contact. Once land was out of reach, navigation became much more difficult; in a featureless expanse of blue, it became necessary to use other guides to find one's way.

Celestial navigation relies on using the sun, moon and stars to establish direction, using those features as reliable points to measure against. These could be simple, such as using the rising or setting sun to chart east and west, or they could be more complex geometric equations measuring the distance from a given star to the horizon. Early examples of celestial navigation are found in **Greek** works, such as Homer's *Odyssey*.

Among the **Polynesian** peoples, open-ocean navigation has a history stretching back around five thousand years. Their art of navigation, also called "*wayfinding*", was based on an understanding of wind and wave patterns as well as the use of celestial navigation. Such techniques were carefully guarded, passed from master to apprentice across generations, and navigators held an elite place of importance in Polynesian society.

Compasses use natural magnetic fields to establish north and south. A compass consists of a lodestone - a piece of magnetite that responds to magnetism - put in a medium where it is capable of moving and turning, such as a basin of water. The lodestone consistently responds to the earth's poles (north or south) and navigation can thus be determined by its angle. Magnetic compasses are generally believed to have originated in **China;** they were generally used to indicate the south, which held significance in Chinese culture. The first definite mention of compasses as a nautical navigation device originates from the *Song* dynasty.

Other devices were used by ancient sailors as well. Among the **Phoenician** peoples (such as those of **Carthage**), sailors would use a bell-shaped lead weight called a *sounding weight* to determine their position. This device would be attached to a rope and dropped into the water. This would measure the depth of the water; furthermore, the device could also collect a small sample of the sea floor. Experienced sailors could use samples to tell their location.

In the medieval **Norse** world, *sunstones* are described in stories such as "*Rauðúlfr's Strand*". Based on their description in such stories, sunstones were transparent crystals that would be held up to the sun on cloudy days. The sunstone would reflect the sun's light even through the cloud, which allowed the sun to be located. This meant the sun could be used for navigation even on overcast days.

VII. ART & AESTHETIC

Artistic design is certainly one of the most visible forms of cultural expression. While the individual's sense of style plays its part, cultural trends can be connected to many aspects of the culture and reflective of their beliefs as a whole. A culture's crafts and artwork are dependent on its resources, its religion, and its values.

7.1 Hair & Body Modification

One of the oldest forms of personal decoration involves hair, whether it's cutting or tying it. Haircuts hold both cultural and utilitarian significance in many cultures, and in some cases the two connect.

Among the **Norse** and **Germanic** peoples, hair was often worn long, with short hair being a sign of slavery. Germanic hair was often bleached, which was noted by Pliny the Elder, and the Muslim scholar Ahmad Ibn Fadlan noted the same thing among the **Rus** people. Bleaching was done with fat and ashes, and in the case of the Germans, was said to give hair a reddish color. Pliny noted that both men and women did it, although the latter more than the former. The Norse were also common users of combs as well as being frequent bathers; the 12th century writer John of Wallingford wrote that because of their cleanliness, *"they laid siege to the virtue of the married woman, and persuaded the daughters even of the noble to be their concubines"*. It should be noted that despite the common image of wild-haired Viking warriors, Norse and Germanic warriors probably tied their hair back in combat, as would most other long-haired warriors throughout history.

The **Germanic** Suebi tribe wore a distinct hairstyle called a *Suebian knot*. Long hair was "knotted" on the upper-side of the head (left or right of the pate). Evidence of this hairstyle exists in contemporary accounts, in artwork and sculpture of the time, and on two preserved heads of Suebian individuals. According to the Roman historian Tacitus, the hairstyle was meant to make the wearer more intimidating and tall, and spread to the warriors of neighboring Germanic peoples.

The **Normans** of northern France were Norsemen who became vassals of the French crown. The Norman haircut was designed to hold one's helmet in place without discomfort. A Norman haircut consists of short hair in the front, top and sides, with an angular swathe cut out on the back. In essence, the back of the head and the area around the ears is shaved to nothing. Normans were also more likely to keep their faces shorn, unlike their northern neighbors.

The **Parikitaru** people of the American midwest, also known as the **Pawnee**, attached cultural value to what is known to modern people as the *mohawk* haircut. In fact, that haircut is what gives the tribe its endonymic name (what the tribe actually calls itself). "Parikitaru" translates to "Split Horned ones", referring to the hairstyle. The *actual* hairstyle of the **Mohawk** people was shared amongst the **Haudenosaunee** peoples and involved hair being pulled (rather than shorn) in every area except the crown of the head. From the remaining hair, braids were fashioned.

Among the **Ukranian Cossacks**, a mohawk-style haircut called a *khokol* (forelock) was often worn. The sides and back of the head were shaved, leaving a central strip. In addition, a lock of long hair was allowed to dangle from the front. This is where the hairstyle gets its name. The term eventually became used as a derogatory name for Ukranians amongst Russians, and then later as a form of self-identification for Ukrainians.

The *chonmage* was a traditional hairstyle among the nobility of **Japan**. Like the Norman haircut, it was designed to keep one's helmet in place comfortably. A chonmage consisted of a shaved pate (top of head). The back and sides were tied up into a small tail that was made to rest atop the shaved pate. This would help hold one's helmet steady. However, even after the samurai stopped having military value, the haircut was maintained as a traditional concept. It was also worn by sumo wrestlers, and in modern times, sumo wrestlers are the only common wearers of the style.

In the ancient periods of Japanese history, hair was often depicted as being worn in *mizura*, which is two tied bunches on the side of the head. Some sources - such as the contemporary novel *The Tale of Genji* - made it seem that this style was only worn by young boys. However, other findings, such as tombs and statues from the time, indicate that the style, or a similar style, was also worn by adult men. Some records suggest that nobles had longer loops on their mizura, while peasants had shorter. Women had more diverse hair options, but the most common was hair drawn back and up into a raised bun called a *shimada mage*.

In the **Valencia** region of **Spain**, a hairstyle called a *fallera* is worn by women for the "Falles" festival, at least in modern times. The haircut consists of two "side-buns" and one "back-bun", ornamented heavily with jewelry. The hairstyle corresponds to *The Lady of Eix*, a bust from the 4th century BC depicting a Celt-Iberian noblewoman or priestess.

Namibia's **Himba** people use hairstyle as a marker of social status. Children have their heads shorn. As they age, braided plaits of hair are added to their heads - a single one for a boy, and two for a girl. These braids are held in place with *ojitze*, a compound of milk-fat and ochre, giving the hair a clay-like coloring and appearance. Women add many plaits as they grow older, arranged based on their clan. A woman who has been married for a year, or who has given birth to a child, adds a sheepskin headdress called an *Erembe* to her everyday wear. Men retain their single plait, but cover their hair under a cap if they get married.

For men, facial hair was often an important aspect of their style that connected to their masculinity and virility. The beards of wealthy **Mesopotamian** peoples (including the **Assyrians** and **Babylonians**) were often intricately braided, creating a knotted look with relatively even edges. These beards may also have been waxed at the ends, and different styles may have been a marker of different classes. Beards were the most dominant around 3000 BCE; art from the same region a millennium later depicts less beards and more shaven faces.

Among the **Celtic** peoples, facial hair is described as being mustache-centric, often without lower beards. The Greek historian Diodolus Siculus describes them as follows: "*Some of them shave the beard, but others let it grow a little; and the nobles shave their cheeks, but they let the moustache grow until it covers the mouth. Consequently, when they are eating, their moustaches become entangled in the food, and when they are drinking, the beverage passes, as it were, through a kind of a strainer.*"

The **Greeks** considered facial hair to be a sign of virility (as did many of their neighbors, such as the **Iranians**). Beards were kept long and sometimes curled with hot tongs, although shaving the upper lip was permissible. Shaving the whole beard was done as a sign of mourning, and shaving half of a man's beard was a punishment for cowardice amongst the **Spartans**. The cultural importance of the beard in the Hellenic world was reduced with Alexander the Great of **Macedon**, who not only was clean-shaven himself, but who ordered his soldiers to be clean-shaven so their beards could not be grabbed by foes during a melee.

The **Roman** model was partially the opposite of the Greek, despite the many Hellenic influences on the Roman culture. Romans went clean-shaven most of the time, and any beards they did grow were usually kept trimmed and tidy. Long, unshaven beards were seen either as a sign of untidiness or as a mark of mourning. This eventually changed with the Emperor Hadrian, who grew a beard to hide facial blemishes. As a result of this, beards became stylish and many emperors after Hadrian had beards as well.

One of the tenets of the *Sikh* faith is *Kesh*, which means allowing one's hair to grow freely. This natural style is done out of respect for the creator's beauty. Cutting hair was described by the 10th Sikh Guru as "as sinful as incest". This extends to facial hair for both men and women, which can be startling for those unfamiliar with the faith.

In *Islam*, the beard is considered a necessary part of masculinity, although the mustache region should be shorn or trimmed. This was done in order to represent a reversal of previous beliefs - *"Nafi Ibn Umar (Radiallahu'Anhu) said, The Prophet Muhammad (Peace Be Upon Him) said, 'Do the opposite of what the pagans do. Keep the beards and cut the mustaches short.'"* This indicates that other, polytheistic **Arabs** of that period shaved their beards and kept their mustaches long.

133

Tattooing and body painting have long histories stretching back to the earliest days of human culture. They use one of the most readily-available canvases - the human body - as a medium for artistic expression.

Tattoos have been found on mummies of women, and images of women, from ancient **Egypt**. Some of these tattoos were religious in nature, being connected to goddesses like Hathor (who represented fertility). Their neighbors, the **Nubians**, shared this practice as evidenced by archaeological finds of tattooed women. Images of tattooed Egyptian men have been found, but no remains thus far have been discovered.

The ancient peoples of southeast Europe - the **Dacians**, **Thracians** and **Illyrians** - were known for their use of body tattooing. These peoples were considered barbarians by their southern Greek neighbors, but naturally had a complex culture of their own. Their tattoos are not well-recorded, but based on writings of the time it seems as though the tattoos themselves had to do with status, either reflecting it or providing it.

In **Japan**, ritual tattooing was practiced both by the aboriginal peoples (the **Jomon** people, who became the **Emishi** and **Ainu**), as well as the **Yamato** people who would eventually become the "modern" Japanese. For both groups tattooing had spiritual elements. Eventually, tattooing amongst the Yamato gained a stigma and was only done by (or in many cases, *to*) criminals, marking their status. Amongst the aboriginal groups, however, it maintained its spiritual purpose. For the Ainu, tattooing was done only *by* women and *to* women. Tattoos manifested most obviously on the lips, although the arms were also commonly tattooed. Ainu tattoos played important religious roles, protecting the body from infection and evil spirits. In the 1880s the Japanese government outlawed Ainu tattooing, which was a major spiritual issue for the Ainu and was circumvented whenever possible.

The **Amazigh** people of north Africa tattoo for similar reasons as the Ainu. Tattoos have different meanings and values based on their design (reflecting aspects of nature), and like the Ainu they are generally placed near openings in the body to protect the body from harmful spirits. Like the Ainu, the Amazigh were discouraged from their practice by a foreign body; *Sunni Islam* prohibits tattooing, and the practice is currently in the process of dying out.

The people of **Samoa** have a ritualized form of tattooing, which is called *pe'a*. A pe'a is an intricate, heavily detailed tattoo going from the waist down to the knees. The density of the tattoo's design combined with the low-tech methods used to ink it means that a pe'a is incredibly painful to receive and it takes a long time as well. As a result, a pe'a is used by both men as a symbol of strength and determination. A male Samoan who has recieved a pe'a is known as a *soga'imiti*; in older times, being a soga'imiti was a prerequisite for being a *matai*, or chief. Women can also receive tattoos that grant cultural boons; these are called *malu*, and are much lighter and less dense than the pe'a.

Skin-carving (*tā moko*) plays an important role in the culture of the **Maori** people, who inhabit New Zealand. Tā moko is done by using bone chisels to groove the skin, and then coloring those grooves with pigments made from burnt timber and the *awheto* fungus. Tā moko patterns involve detailed spirals which are distinct and unique between individuals. Men receive it across their entire face, as well as parts of the lower body. Women receive it on their lips and chin, as well as the lower body. Tā moko is a distinct cultural product of the Maori people, and they consider it offensive to have it done on a non-Maori. However, "designs with Maori flavor" done with ink instead of carving are considered acceptable.

In **Thailand** and **Vietnam**, a practice called *yantra* tattooing has a 2000-year history. Yantra is a concept from Indian religions such as Hinduism and Buddhism that associates power and significance with certain icons and geometric shapes. Yantra tattooing imbues the wearer with powers based on their shape and design as long as they maintain religious beliefs consistent with the blessing. The *wai khru* ritual is a yearly occasion for students to pay respect and show gratitude for their teachers; during this time, tattoos are usually repaired in order to maintain their power.

As for the body itself, every culture has its own standards of beauty that determine their "ideal" body, as well as local conditions that determine the *actual* body type commonly found in the region. When I say "ideal" it is important, as always, to remind the reader that individuals have their own preferences, but what we are discussing is general trends and patterns across societal groups.

In 1951, Clellan Ford and Frank Beach published a book called *Patterns of Sexual Behavior*, an anthropological study of different cultures examining sexual mores and beauty standards. Their conclusion was that there are relatively few universal standards of beauty, although it was noted that almost all cultures pay more attention to criteria for female attractiveness than for male.

Within their study group, most societies preferred plump women, with slim and "moderate" tying for second place. Societies with a preference for larger women included the **Wogeo** of Oceania, the **Nama** people of southern Africa, and the **Baganda** people of Uganda. Societies with a preference for thinner women include the **Masai** of east Africa, the **Palaung** people of southeast Asia, and the **Chenchu** of India. Most societies responded positively to a "broad pelvis and wide hips", with only one (the **Yakut** people of northeast Russia) indicating revulsion at this and a preference for the opposite. Large breasts were commonly considered desirable, but two cultures (the Baganda and the **Azande** of the Congo) specifically preferred "long, pendulous" breasts, while the Masai and the **Manus** of Papua New Guinea preferred smaller "upright, hemispherical" breasts. Certain cultures outside the study were noted as having a preference for smaller breasts, such as the ancient **Greeks**, **Romans** and **Japanese**.

Male attractiveness in most cultures was generally derived from fitness and athleticism. The **Greeks**, as discussed earlier, had a strong homosexual component to their culture, and naturally they had some strong opinions on the male body. Specifically, small penises were preferred to large ones, which were commonly used as the butt of jokes or gags. Male bodies were idealized as muscular and fit. In artwork, even when youthful beauty was being represented, it was usually attached to a well-developed physique.

In **Chinese** culture, male attractiveness is depicted as important less often than other virtues. However, the depiction of attractiveness itself tends to oscillate between strong muscular men and weak beautiful men. For example, the 6th century figure Gao Changgong was famous for his beautiful features, which he hid with a mask in battle. The *Jin* dynasty's Wei Jie attracted crowds of women wherever he went with his delicate features. He died at 27 years old, and the reason why (recorded in the *Book of Jin*) was a complication of "being looked at too much". With the *Tang* dynasty (beginning 618 CE), strong features and masculinity regained importance, but in the *Ming* era (1368 CE), handsomeness gave way to beauty once again.

People in many societies (usually women) would use makeup to accentuate their features. *Kohl* is an ancient cosmetic used by **Egyptians, Indians, Ethiopians, Hausa, Tuareg, Amazighen, Arabs,** and many other cultures from west Africa to southeast Asia. It is made of ground stibnite (a grey-black mineral) and was applied around the eyes. Makeup, used to color the skin, could be made out of either mineral or plant components. Skin-whitening was done in several societies, including **Greek, English** and **Japanese**. Earlier, it was mentioned that the **Himba** people of Namibia use *ojitze* - a mixture of milk-fat and ochre - to style their hair. In addition to this, they also use it as a skin covering to protect against sun and insects. The reddish shade that it gives to the skin is considered beautiful among the Himba, being symbolic of the earth and blood.

In **China**, the practice of foot-binding began with upper-class women in the 10th century and eventually spread to women of all social classes. It involved tightly binding women's feet from an early age in order to stunt their growth. This created small, delicate appendages that necessitated the "Lotus gait", a swaying method of walking that was considered erotically appealing. Bound feet (also called Lotus feet) were deformed and damaged, resulting in health conditions for the women whose feet were bound. Some Chinese writers indicated that such feet were only beautiful when they were hidden behind shoes or fabric. Bound feet also reduced a woman's practical mobility, meaning that they became more passive and dependent on men.

Some other societies practice similar acts of body-modification for female beauty. The **Kayan** people of Burma place stiff metal rings around women's necks from an early age. This gives them a long neck that is considered attractive in adulthood. A similar practice is used by the **Southern Ndebele** people of southern Africa, although in this case the practice is a symbol of marriage, rather than being done from youth. As a result the effect is sometimes less extreme.

Certain cultures use *lip plates* for personal decoration. This involves piercing the lip and inserting an object in order to open it, in a manner akin to spacer earrings or "gauges". Cultures that engaged in this practice include the **Suya**, **Botocudo** and **Zo'e** of Brazil, the **Mursi** and **Suri** of Ethiopia, the **Aleut**, **Inuit** and **Haida** of the American northwest, the **Sara** of central Africa, and the **Makonde** of southeast Africa.

Dying one's teeth black was a practice found across many parts of east Asia. In **Japan**, it was called *ohaguro* and was practiced by the nobility (men and women) from its earliest history up to the late 1800s. Details regarding the original purpose of the act are unknown, but it is known that the dye acts as a form of dental sealant, and also that shiny black items (such as lacquered items) were considered particularly beautiful. The practice is also found amongst many minority peoples in China, Thailand, Vietnam and the Pacific Islands. The **Dai** people of southern China are probably the most numerous, with the **Hmong** and **Yao** as second and third most, respectively.

7.2 Clothing

Clothing is one of the most immediately-visible aspects of a cultural group. In everyday life it serves a practical as well as visual purpose; people dress for utilitarian reasons, but also for style and fashion. In most cases, utility comes *first*, and *then* style is layered onto that. Exceptions to the rule are generally related to higher-ranking peoples who do not need as much utility out of their clothing. When discussing the utility of clothing, first we must talk about climate. When designing your culture, remember that most regions of the world alternate dramatically between hot and cold, and thus your culture should have a broad array of clothing options to account for this.

In *hot, dry* weather, skin coverage is essential. Clothing is incredibly important for keeping the sun off the body, but it must be done without trapping heat. As a result, peoples such as the **Amazigh**, **Bedouin**, **Arabs** and **Iranians** generally wear large garments made of light, breathable materials such as linen or cotton. While they share "coverage" with cold-weather clothing, hot-dry clothing tends to be more "billowing" in nature, to allow for air to pass through them.

In *hot, wet* weather, cloth coverage becomes less important. Cloth over skin combined with humidity leads to uncomfortable stickiness. Ventilation is very important. The average **Roman** citizen living in the Mediterranean region would wear only a *tunica* belted at the waist, along with sandals. The **Greeks** had a similar garment, the *chiton*. Their forebears, the **Minoans**, had loincloths or short skirts for both men and women - a similar situation existed in ancient **India** and **Egypt**. Sandals and shoes existed primarily to protect the feet, whereas in colder climates footwear also needed to provide warmth. Gloves would be worn for certain special purposes (i.e. keeping hands clean during eating) but not in general life.

Both the Greeks and Romans encountered trouser-wearing cultures, but for both cultures they were thought of as strange and ridiculous. Unlike the Greeks, the Romans eventually spread their empire to colder climates, and thus were forced to adopt trousers for utilitarian reasons.

This adoption was itself considered barbaric by Romans further south. In later Roman culture, trousers were worn even in the southern parts of the empire. For example, the people of the **Eastern Roman Empire**, also known as the **Byzantine Empire**, wore trousers even though they lived in the same Mediterranean climate as their forebears.

In <u>cold</u> weather, layering becomes important, and the colder it is, the more layers are necessary. Multiple layered tunics were used to protect the torso, usually with cloaks or similar garments (capes, mantles, etc.) over all. As mentioned, trousers or pants were originally a cold-weather invention, worn by **Celts**, **Germans**, and peoples of the **Iranian** region (including **Scythians** and **Armenians**). Shoes and boots were a necessity, and were sometimes lined with wool or fur for extra warmth. Socks or leg-wrappings are documented as being somewhat uncommon, but were of major benefit when hiking through snow or cold, marshy areas. Hats or hoods were also important, although long hair and beards could at least partially take their place. Gloves were valuable but relatively difficult to manufacture, and they did not show up in common usage (in Europe at least) until the 1000s.

Unlike hot-dry clothing, cold weather clothing clung tightly to the body in order to preserve heat. Wool was considered an excellent cold-weather material, as was fur. Linen was used, but generally had to be layered to be effective. The general patterns described here are true for the **Germanic** peoples, the **Norse**, the **Sami** of Finland, the **Celts** (including the **Britons** and **Picts**), the people of **Nepal** and **Tibet**, and so on.

There are some cases where societies are forced to make do with only a few of those elements due to resource limitations. For example, the **Inuit** peoples of North America were too far north to reliably grow crops or raise animals. As a result, they were limited entirely to hunted pelts and furs for their clothing.

Once the utilitarian concerns are taken care of, then the aesthetic aspects of clothing design can be introduced. Almost every culture in the world took some level of visual pride in their clothing, as a status symbol or as a form of expression. Clothing aesthetics are expressed through *coloring, patterning, layering* and *accessorization.*

Coloring refers to the base colors used in the item of clothing. The colors that can be used are determined by the availability of dyes, which is a substance applied to cloth or fabric that permanently changes its color. Dye can be plant-based, animal-derived, or mineral-based. Every method would generally produce only a single color. For example, in **Navajo** society, the prickly pear cactus is fermented in order to make a pinkish-red color. In South America, the *añil* plant is used for indigo coloration. *Ochre* is a clay material used as a primitive yellow dye, as well as for painting. The famous shade of "royal purple" was derived from sea snails, and the process of harvesting it was so cumbersome that it was intensely expensive to obtain. As a result, that particular shade of purple became known as the color of royalty, although "lesser" purples could be obtained by the mixing of red and blue dyes.

Most cultures have their own ideas about which colors go with which *other* colors. This is called "color theory", and the goal of it is "color harmony". Color harmony is often dependent on a given color's relation to other colors on the color wheel. However, it is also highly subjective in nature, based on certain cultures' associations with shades or hues. In ancient Egypt, the color blue was associated with divinity. In Rome, however, it was associated with mourning, as well as lower-class clothing. These sorts of meanings are specific to societies and will influence their usage in fashion.

Patterning is the use of embellishments and designs on clothing. In some cases this may be limited to the borders, or "hems", of clothing. In other cases, such as the *tartan* pattern, it affects the entire piece of clothing. Such patterns are generally repeated to create a sense of uniformity. Patterning is not necessarily technology-intensive, but without certain tools it *is* labor-intensive. As a result, patterned clothing throughout history is generally associated with the upper classes, while the lower classes make do with plain clothing.

The use of certain symbols on clothing (and architecture, and handicrafts, and so on) is common across the world. These patterns could be individually placed, or they could be a repeating pattern. Repeating patterns often attempt to invoke symbolism through geometry, such as mountains, waves, scales, or spirals. Some examples of distinct, non-repeating symbols include the **Celtic** *triskeles*, the **French** *fleur des lis*, the **Georgian** *borjgali*, and the **Germanic** *dragon's eye* and *valknut*. Noble families would also often have their own symbols, which would be worn by family members or retainers; examples include the **Japanese** *mon*, **European** *coat of arms*, and the **Scottish** *clan crest*.

For many cultures, certain patterns or symbols hold talisman-like protective patterns. One well-used **Turkish** pattern is the *elibelinde*, a female figure with her hands on her hips. This pattern represents fertility and motherhood. Triangles were used to represent protective amulets. Horn-like patterns were meant to represent masculinity. Among the **Navajo**, rugs were a garment as well as a blanket. They are often woven with *storm patterns*, though the symbolism and meaning of individual patterns tends to vary by the artist.

Tartan, or plaid, patterning was common in the **Celtic** and **Gaelic** world. In **Scotland**, tartan clothing eventually became controversial because it represented Gaelic culture, and thus was perceived as "anti-English". Some tartan patterns were associated with specific areas of Scotland, but this was more because of materials availability (dyes, for example) than cultural values. However, in the 19th century, King George IV visited Scotland and began an **English** craze that romanticized the tartan and Gaelic identity. To profit off this, tartan manufacturers in Scotland essentially created "clan tartans" - a fictional historical institution connecting certain tartan patterns to certain clans. Despite a lack of evidence for their historical presence, clan tartans took off in popularity and were eventually accepted as fact. This is an example of an "invented tradition".

Layering is the juxtaposition or correlation of individual items of clothing to create a visual "whole". Again, the concept of color harmony comes into play, as do contrasting patterns. Layering also serves a practical purpose, shielding the wearer from cold or dampness. Even in warm, dry climates, however, layering is done for visual reasons.

Common outer garments are cloaks, capes, jackets, ponchos, shawls or raincoats (such as the *mino*, a **Japanese** straw cloak). Such garments were held together by rope (the cheaper method) or with metal pins or brooches. **Norse** women wore an apron-like garment called a *hangerock* over their dresses. The **Iranian** *kandys* was a long garment somewhere between a robe and a coat, but with intentionally overlong sleeves. As such, it was generally worn as a cloak, with arms out of the sleeves. The sleeves were reserved for court presentation, where they may have been used as a security assurance (i.e. ensuring the nobles were too clumsy or tied-up to do anything dangerous).

Undergarments were made of comfortable materials such as linen, and were generally undyed. Loincloths could be found across most cultures as a lower covering. **European** men, including **Celts**, **Germans** and **Norse**, wore shirts and tights (*braies*) under their clothes if they could afford them. Robe-like garments such as the **Japanese** *kimono* or **Chinese** *hanfu* often had an undyed garment as their bottom layer. Women would sometime wear breast-supporting garments, such as the **Indian** *kanchuka* or **Greek** *strophia*, which was a set of leather straps worn over clothes. Certain finds suggest that Norse women also wore bras with metal components. In some cases, breasts were least "supported" and more "bound". The **Roman** *fascia* was designed to prevent women's breasts from growing too large, as large breasts were considered unsightly. The **Japanese** *sarashi* was a cloth strip wound tightly around the torso by both men and women; for women, however, it served both a practical purpose (limiting breast movement) and an aesthetic one.

Layered clothing also has aesthetic value when combined with military gear, such as armor. While armor itself is often visually "monochrome", the use of layering over and under the armor can create a more distinct look. It also has the benefit of being able to convey allegiance and heraldry. In Medieval **Europe**, this was accomplished with *surcoats*. In **Japan**, the *jinbaori* played a similar role. Across the world this effect was accomplished with cloaks, capes, coats, tabards, mantles, skirts, and similar items. A form of armor existed that actually put armor plating between cloth, allowing it to be worn itself as "normal clothing" and designed accordingly. This armor was called *brigandine* in Europe, *chihal'ta hazar masha* in **India**, *dingjia* in **China**, *kuyak* in **Russia**, and *kikko* in Japan.

The *Knights Hospitaller* wore a full monk's robe with their armor, because of their dual role as monks and knights. In 1248, Pope Innocent IV granted them a specific garb to be worn in battle - this was done because their traditional costume was considered too restrictive by the knights themselves. Note, too, that this permission was only granted during battle itself; in all other circumstances, they were required to wear their traditional garb.

Accessorization is the use of other garb, such as jewelry, belts, pouches, bags and totems to complete the design. It is arguably the oldest of the four aspects, as primitive, hand-made jewelry dates to before any sort of dyeing.

Jewelry refers to necklaces, bracelets, rings, earrings, and brooches or clasps. While the name typically calls to mind precious metals and gemstones, it is not a necessity. Early jewelry consisted of shells, beads, feathers or carved antler/tusk looped on woven textiles or animal sinew. Later jewelers would occasionally include such materials for visual effect. Jewelry made of more precious materials was used as a sign of wealth and prestige, while simpler handmade jewelry was used by many people as a personal affectation.

The **Celts**, **Scythians**, **Thracians** and **Illyrians** were fond of neck-rings known as *torcs*, which were often used to identify the status of the wearer. Torcs were usually made of gold (if possible) and bronze (if not). Some torcs were made in elaborate "twisted" patterns. Some appear to have been designed so that they would be worn permanently (or, at least, it would be difficult to remove them).

Amulets and *totems* were jewelry-like items of religious importance, often used to safeguard the wearer or bring luck. These items can range in value from casual superstition to deep, important religious belief.

Among *Christians*, the *crucifix* has been said to carry protective powers from the origins of the faith. Beginning in the 11th century, another amulet was introduced - the *Saint Benedict Medal*, which was (and is) said to carry "devil-chasing" powers. The view of the modern Roman Catholic Church is that these items are powered by their faith, not by any intrinsic magical ability. In *Judaism*, the *Seal of Solomon* - a six-pointed pentagram - carries a similar protective value. The *tefillin*, a black leather box containing Torah parchment, is strapped to the arm or forehead for certain religious rituals.

An *omamori* is a **Japanese** talisman consisting of a tab of wood or paper wrapped in silk. The talisman is made sacred at a Shinto or Buddhist shrine and (at least in modern times) serves a particular purpose, such as family health, financial luck, or repelling evil. In more ancient times, an earthen or jade bead called a *magatama* was common. Its purpose was often unclear even with mythological examples of its "usage". In one story, a dog kills a badger (considered mythical) and discovers a magatama in its stomach. The magatama is then enshrined at a holy site. The reasons why are unclear; it was perhaps considered self-evident enough during the period to be not worth explaining.

In **Egypt**, especially in the Middle Kingdom (2000 BCE), scarab beetles were a popular shape for amulets. These amulets were produced in large numbers and were worn by a great number of people. The symbolism involved was related to the god Khepri, an aspect of Ra the Sun God responsible for rolling the sun across the sky. In this way, a scarab talisman may have represented rebirth or the cycle of life. Another, older talisman from Egypt (and also **Mesopotamia**) was the *cylinder seal*, a cylinder made of hardstones or gems like hematite that was engraved a depiction with a historical or mythical event. Such seals were often worn as necklaces and could be used to stamp (or roll) an image onto wet clay.

In **Turkey**, an amulet called the *nazar* is meant to ward off the "evil eye", a curse transmitted by a malevolent glare. The amulet itself depicts an eye, often with a blue iris (because blue and green eyes, in real life, are thought to be more capable of transmitting the curse). Belief in the evil eye goes back to Classical **Greece**, and was spread by Alexander the Great. Other cultures have similar totems against it. An icon called the *hamsa*, depicting a hand with an eye on its palm, is used by both *Jews* and *Muslims*, but is said to have its origins in **Carthaginian** paganism. In **Italy**, a slightly twisted horn symbol called a *cornicello* (little horn) is used.

In **Ethiopia**, a small manuscript is wrapped up in leather to form a charm called a *kitab*, which is worn on a beaded necklace. In **Ghana**, a similar item called a *gris-gris* exists, although the manuscript contains excerpts of the Koran, and the wrapping is cloth.

In the north of **India**, the term *"nazarbattu"* is used for an almost indescribable range of icons, totems and designs meant to ward off the evil eye. The nazarbattu is, itself, an "imperfection"; for example, a parent may make a mark on their child's cheek as a form of nazarbattu. This is because the evil eye is said to be attracted to "excessive admiration" or perfection.

In **Tibet**, talismans made of meteoric iron (*thokcha*, or "sky-iron") are said to possess magical protective powers. Such metals are said to have been tempered by celestial deities. In some cases thokcha items were used for more practical purposes, such as harnesses or buckles, but they retained their protective power in this role. Another Tibetan amulet was the *dzi*, a stone bead decorated with protective symbols.

7.3 Literature & Storytelling

Storytelling is the act of creating fictional narratives. There are three reasons that storytelling is done, and the three often intertwine in the same stories. The first reason is to give information, the second is to convey morals and values, and the third is to evoke emotional states. Storytelling can be done through a variety of mediums, from oral recital to theatrical productions to the written word. Regardless of the medium, the core purposes are the same.

First is the topic of <u>explanatory storytelling</u>: stories that purport to give information about the world. Stories like this are recited, often as part of oral tradition, to provide information about the way things are and how they got that way. Stories of this variety were designed to answer natural questions about the world and generally had some sort of religious or cultural slant to them.

One type of explanatory story is the *porquoi* story (French for "but why?"), also known as the "just so" story. These are stories that purport to explain some facet of nature with a fable or mythological origin. Such stories are at the very foundation of culture, and every society across the globe and throughout time has had some variant of it. In **Greek** myth, the story of Persephone is used to explain why winter occurs. **Mesopotamian** culture had a similar story to explain the same phenomenon - that of Ishtar and her husband Dumuzi. In **Norse** myth, the god Loki was eventually bound beneath the earth for his misdeeds, with a serpent perpetually dripping venom onto his face. His wife dutifully catches the poison in a bowl, but when the poison hits him, he writhes in pain. This was used to explain earthquakes.

One sub-set of explanatory stories are creation myths, which specifically explain how existence as a whole came to be. Just as almost every culture has its own set of porquoi stories, almost every culture also has a creation myth. Many creation myths begin with a void in which a creator deity builds reality from nothingness (*ex nihilo*). Others have reality existing as a chaotic mess that a deity brings to order. An alternative is that "reality" is a union between powerful beings, such as **Greek** myth, where Gaia (the earth) unites with her offspring Uranus (the sky) and Pontus (the sea) to create the world.

An alternative to the creation myth is the national origin myth. This does not explain the origins of the world, but explains the origins of the culture and how it came to exist. For example, the **Choctaw** people relate a story where two brothers led their tribe from a land that had become barren. They used a magical staff to guide their passage; they would place it in the ground, and it would lean to determine their next destination. When they finally reached a place where it stood straight up, they buried the bones of their ancestors at its base. This created a sacred mound of earth called *Nanih Waiya*. The area was not fertile enough to support all the people gathered, so one brother split his followers off and formed the **Chickasaw** tribe, while the other brother and his followers remained as the Choctaw.

A common explanatory archetype relates to the origin of death. Probably the most famous is the **Greek** story of Pandora's Box, but such stories are common in Africa, America, and Oceania. In such stories, humans are naturally immortal, but lose their immortality as the result of hubris or bad luck. An alternative is the **Polynesian** story of the hero Māui, who attempts to stop death by overcoming the Great Woman of the Night. He did this by crawling into her womb, up through her mouth, thus reversing the process of birth and death. However, one of his companions laughed at the ridiculousness of the task, waking the Great Woman and leading to Māui's death. The **Baganda** people of Uganda have a god of death named Walumbe. Walumbe is the son of Ggulu, the creator. When his sister Nambi is won as a bride by Kintu, the original human, Walumbe follows the pair from heaven to earth, and thus brings mortality to their descendants.

Second is moral storytelling. Moral storytelling exists to convey heroic values, to establish a culture's idea of what "being a hero" means. It creates an ideal for people to imitate and live up to, a function still found in modern stories. The protagonists of such stories could be flawed or tragic in their own ways, but this could be used to dramatically illustrate what they had done wrong, and through this establish what the "right" path was.

The most obvious and overt kind of moral storytelling are *fables*, such as the ones famously made by the **Greek** writer Aesop. These are generally perceived as stories for children meant to illustrate basic values. In such tales, morality has consequences that are meant to be understandable and relatable in simple ways. For example, in the story of "the Grasshopper and the Ant", hard work is rewarded while idleness is punished in a very unmistakable way. Many fables across cultures have similar elements and lessons. The *Aarne-Thompson-Uther* classification system is a scholarly tool used to categorize recurring themes across cultures. One can compare stories such as the Grimm brothers' "The Fisherman and his Wife" to the **Japanese** "The Stonecutter". Both were about people from humble origins who seek more and more. However, in the former, the individuals' greed is endless and they are eventually punished by the being that gave them power in the first place. In the latter, the stonecutter realizes that he is not truly happy in any of those positions, and becomes content with his place in the world. These differences serve as a reflection of cultural values and the moral lesson that is being taught.

Sometimes, more complex stories can be used to develop cultural values. In the **Anglo-Saxon** story *Beowulf*, the titular hero represented the ideal man in their culture. He is strong, brave and indomitable. He challenges the monstrous Grendel, who has slain many armed warriors, while Beowulf himself fights naked and unarmed. While fighting Grendel's mother, he lifts a giant's sword, described as something only he could have done. In addition to his exaggerated acts of heroism, Beowulf also connects to many more relatable values; he is a champion of many Anglo-Saxon sports, including swimming and wrestling, which prepares him for his duties in combat. After slaying Grendel's mother, Beowulf is rewarded by King Hrothgar, who takes the opportunity to remind Beowulf of the values of rulership, such as generosity and a good reputation. Beowulf's story exists in many ways to propagate an ideal value for Anglo-Saxons to work towards, and cultural lessons are intertwined with the story.

In medieval **Europe**, the *romance* genre developed as a way to encourage values such as chivalry, nobility, and courtly love. Such works were often based on history, albeit exaggerated, such as the stories of King Arthur and his knights (*The Matter of Britain*) or Charlemagne and his paladins (*The Matter of France*). From those stories, idealized heroes like Roland, Lancelot and Percival were contrasted against more "normal", mortal knights, or against the villainy and treachery of their enemies. Romance stories also, naturally, had a strong Christian element, with their heroes being pious and upholding virtue and valor. Even these mighty heroes could often be tempted by material sins, making them relatable to audiences but also clearly illustrating the results of their weakness.

In the ancient **Indian** epic, the *Mahabharata*, there is a key scene where the hero, Arjuna, is conferring with his chariot driver, who is secretly the god Krishna. Arjuna expresses his concerns to Krishna; he is pitted against his own family and friends as part of a climactic conflict of inheritance, and loathes the violence to follow. Krishna's answer to these concerns is to emphasize the virtue of fulfilling one's role without attachment to results. He reveals the true cosmic scale of the universe, and how the nature of devotion and faith are more important than temporary physical concerns. This exchange, the *Bhagavad Gita*, is an extended lesson in Hindu philosophy that provides complex and intricate lessons for its reader.

The final aspect of stories is evocative storytelling. This refers to the emotional impact that stories are meant to have. Evocative techniques were usually intertwined with explanatory or moral storytelling as a way of making the subject more palatable. The word "evocative" here means that a work was designed to elicit emotional response, whether that response was laughter, excitement, sadness, or anger. People take part in works of entertainment in order to be emotionally affected.

The *Natya Shastra* was an **Indian** treatise on theatre and performance dating from somewhere between 200 BCE and 200 CE. In addition to instructions on stagecraft and presentation, it dealt with the "Nine *Rasas*", or moods. These were as follows: romance, comedy, fury, compassion, disgust, horror, heroism, amazement and tranquility. Indian art and theatre was often based on intentionally and selectively appealing to these emotions. However, the Natya Shastra also identifies drama as an important tool for religious instruction, connecting it back to explanatory and moral storytelling.

In **Greek** theater, the two main emotional states were tragedy and comedy. The two states were kept separate from each other, and few works attempted to include both emotional states. In his *Poetics*, the philosopher Aristotle wrote that "*Comedy aims at representing men as worse, Tragedy as better than in actual life*". Furthermore, comedy was "*ugly and distorted*", but not "*painful or destructive*", which would change the mood. Tragedy, on the other hand, was "*imitation of an action that is serious, complete, and of a certain magnitude*". Its role was "cathartic"; Aristotle refers to tragedy "purging emotions". In short, comedy was meant to be grotesque and funny, while tragedy was meant to be serious and evocative. Theater as a whole had a strong religious element to it; Many works of Greek theater - comedic or tragic - were meant to convey some greater moral message, as well.

The oldest novel written is the **Japanese** *Tale of Genji*, written in the 11th century by noblewoman Murasaki Shikibu. The novel centers around a story of courtly intrigue, and was written for an audience of female noblewomen. Its primary purpose was to enthrall; the titular Genji is an anti-hero, rather than a moral paragon. The novel also has the structure of a chronicle or historical record, rather than a more traditional story arc. A later form of Japanese storytelling, called *rakugo*, was invented by Buddhist monks in the 9th and 10th century to make their sermons more engaging. Eventually, it evolved into a more secular form as pure entertainment.

In some cases, recurring story patterns designed to elicit a certain emotion could be found across many cultures. For example, "The

Hero's Journey" documented by Joseph Campbell begins with a weak, mundane protagonist who develops strength and character until he can overcome his powerful enemy. In this way, the story structure connects with normal people (i.e. the likely audience) by implicitly connecting them to a powerful mythos. Different types of heroes are meant to appeal to different values and audiences; some defeat enemies through brute strength, while others use trickery or guile.

7.4 Artwork

Discussing art (here defined as "illustration, painting, sculpture, and similar works") is a complicated and imprecise process. While there are obviously cultural trends that can be analyzed, artwork is about subjective responses and individual styles. For this reason it is easier to talk about specific trends within historical artwork rather than styles themselves.

There are several types of artwork. Some of them will not be discussed here because they have been discussed in other parts of this book. For example, tapestry and embroidery are illustrated cloth works that are covered by the topic of looms and weaving. Jewelry and talismans are covered by the section on clothing. What we have left, therefore, are items that exist on their own.

Painting involves applying paint to a surface. Paint is made of pigments (coloring agents), resin (which holds the pigments together and bonds them to the surface), and other chemicals which add desirable properties. Pigments are generally taken from clay or certain types of metal, while resin could be made from eggs, beeswax, casein (taken from milk), or gum arabic. As with clothes, the dyes and pigments available determined the color palette available for painting. The earliest painting surfaces were stone walls, originating with natural cave paintings using red, white and black pigments (taken from clay, calcite and charcoal respectively). The **Egyptians** commonly made use of plastered walls as a superior surface for painting. In **Greece**, painting was often done on pots and other ceramic works; the distinctive style of black-on-orange (with other colors for accentuation) is known as "black figure pottery". Softer, more portable materials included cloth, silk, paper, papyrus and parchment. Silk and paper both originated in **China** and spread outwards from there to **Japan**, **Tibet**, **Vietnam**, and on.

Sculptures are figures or objects made of stone, metal, wood, ceramics, or other solid materials. Sculptures constitute some of the oldest-preserved works of art alongside cave paintings. They could range from hand-held figurines to massive constructions such as the Colossus of Rhodes. Some sculptures were exaggerated figures, while others could be amazingly realistic and detailed. According to Gombrich's "The History of Art", one innovation between the **Egyptians** and the **Greeks** was that the Egyptians sculpted with soft, static poses, while the Greeks became increasingly adventurous in terms of designing "action poses" or passionate faces. Many sculptures, such as those of the Greeks and **Romans**, were painted with garish colors. However, those colors eventually washed off, leaving later cultures to interpret them as intentionally monochromatic - and therefore, stoic and austere. Sculptures made during the **Italian** Renaissance were done in imitation of classical sculptures, and because of this misperception, they were left blank and austere.

Engraving is the process of carving an image into a base of metal, wood or stone (including gemstone). Apart from their distinct visual value, engraving also provided a relatively unique result: a 3d image on a mostly-2d plane. This meant that engraved items could be used for replication purposes. For example, a cylinder seal was a small cylinder that could be rolled across clay to leave an impression. This act did not "use up" the cylinder in any way, and thus it could be done over and over. They were somewhat common in **Iran** and **Mesopotamia**. Another form of engraved replication was woodblock printing, originating in **China**'s Han dynasty. These woodblocks were dipped in ink and then pressed onto paper, a recent invention of the period. This was used to transcribe images and text. This spread to **Korea** and **Japan** shortly thereafter, to the **Arab** world by the 11th century, and to **Europe** by the 14th. The practical aspects of woodblock printing eventually evolved through the use of movable text, which allowed for the assembly of new sentences or works through the arrangement of pre-made components (i.e. letters or characters). This originated in 11th century China, but arguably had more of an impact when it was developed independently and separately in 15th century **Germany**. One major difference between the two was that the German language has many fewer characters than Chinese languages do, allowing for easier message assembly.

Reliefs have elements of both sculptures and engraving, but are intrinsically attached to walls or other solid surfaces. Reliefs can be done in many ways, from the shallow *bas-relief* to the more extruding *high relief* to the carved-in *sunk relief* commonly used by the **Egyptians**. Reliefs have two distinct differences from sculptures. First, they are an architectural feature more than a stand-alone item. Secondly, the space available on a relief's medium generally allows for more complicated and drawn-out scenes akin to a painting, whereas a stand-alone sculpture requires more work for one single image. The Dharmic religions (Hinduism, Buddhism and Jainism) made common use of reliefs on the side of temples; examples can be found in **India**, **Cambodia**, **Thailand**, **Java**, and many other places in southeast Asia.

Reliefs and engravings were sometimes used on *marker structures*, which were made of stone and designed to serve as a long-lasting historical marker. The exact name and nature depends on the culture. The **Norse** erected *runestones* to honor the dead or significant events. These were slabs of rock that were carved with Norse lettering and imagery, and also frequently painted over with hematite-derived red paints. Across **India** can be found similar, more intricate markers known as a *Mahsati* stone (or "Hero stone"). These were designed to honor and depict heroic events, and were generally divided into several "panels" striped horizontally down the length of the stone. The **Romans** would commemorate military campaigns with "triumphal columns". The most well-known of these was the 98-foot-tall Trajan's Column, which (similar to the Mahsati stone) was wrapped around with horizontal panels depicting Trajan's battles and accomplishments. The **Egyptians** raised *tekhenu*, pillars capped with pyramidal points and inscribed with hieroglyphics. The Greeks later referred to these as *obelisks*, which stuck as their most well-known name. Tekhenu were raised for religious reasons, having a connection to the Sun God, Ra. The **Ethiopian** Kingdom of Axum had similar pillars, known as *hawelt*, as markers for royal burial sites. They were designed as false buildings with "windows" and other decorations, and capped with a distinct spade shape.

With regards to painting and illustration, issue of depicting <u>depth and perspective</u> is a surprisingly common one throughout history. While many cultures were wholly capable of creating complex, realistic 3d sculptures or figures, illustrations and paintings throughout history proved to be more troublesome in terms of displaying proper dimensions. In short, most cultures' art showed a flat area, with overlapping items in the field being the only indication of a third dimension. In ancient **Egypt**, a practice called "vertical perspective" was used, where a figure being depicted below another figure meant that the bottom figure was nearer than the top one. The Bayeux Tapestry of 11th century **England** uses a similar technique in certain scenes, usually when a castle is meant to be in the background. In the Morgan Bible, created in 13th century **France**, the majority of images are flat, with occasional inaccurate attempts at perspective when drawing background elements.

Although it was obvious to artists that flat images were inaccurate or unrealistic, attempts at drawing three-dimensional shapes often lacked precision. In Plato's "Republic", Book X, he discussed the issue as part of a larger treatise on the weakness of human perception. In **Greece** and **Rome**, a process called *skenographia* was used to create the illusion of a three-dimensional room, usually as a backdrop for plays. In **China** and **Japan**, the use of oblique perspective (displaying objects at a skewed overhead angle) was used to illustrate cities or landscapes from the 2nd century CE onwards. In **Byzantine** artwork, reverse perspective was sometimes used - in this style, objects that were closer would appear smaller, and objects that were further away would appear larger. A true, mathematically-accurate process of linear perspective was developed in 15th century **Italy** by the painter Fillipo Brunelleschi. By applying geometric theories to observations about horizon lines, he was able to map out the exact patterns of convergence that define true three-dimensional imagery.

Art often had a religious element, allowing viewers to understand and visualize the gods and supernatural beings that existed outside their realm of perception. However, this was not always considered acceptable. <u>Aniconism</u> is the idea of disallowing or rejecting imagery, whether the depiction of religious figures or the depiction of sentient life at all. Religions with aniconistic elements include *Islam*, **Byzantine** *Iconoclasm*, *Calvinism*, the *Amish*, early *Buddhism* (arguably), some pre-Islamic **Iranian** religions, and some **Germanic** tribes. Some forms of aniconism exist either because it is considered inaccurate or even sacrilegious to try to illustrate a god in their "true form". Abrahamic-based aniconism is also rooted in the idea that idols and images are akin to Pagan worship.

In most versions of Islam, there is a strict prohibition against illustrating either God or the Prophet Mohammed, as well as several other high-ranking religious figures. However, there is a more general rule against illustrating life in general that is less strictly enforced. Still, though, this rule had a substantial impact on Islamic art and design. A large amount of Islamic art dispenses with illustration of "reality" entirely, instead focusing on abstract shapes and geometric patterns. Architecture is a common medium for Islamic artwork, with complicated patterning and mosaic-work found on most mosques and palaces.

Christian Iconoclasm shares the core concept of not depicting divine figures, but does not share the same distaste for depicting humans or animals. In the **Byzantine Empire**, the Iconoclast sect believed that saints were the source of too much worship. They felt that this was changing from monotheism, with veneration of relics and saints, to henotheism, where the saints themselves are lesser deities. In such a scenario, veneration of saints would be akin to worshiping another god. For this reason, the Iconoclasts tore down religious imagery throughout the empire. However, they were eventually ousted from power by the pro-image *Iconodules*, who argued that strong imagery played a powerful role in establishing faith.

In early Buddhist artwork, the Buddha himself is rarely represented, according to certain scholarly interpretations. Instead, symbols such as the *dharma wheel*, the *bodhi tree*, or an empty throne are used in his place. However, this interpretation is disputed, and such images are thought to be showing the objects themselves (as a symbol of worship for pilgrims and adherents) rather than being a stand-in for the Buddha.

The **Scythian** people, according to Herodotus, worshiped a war god (described as a "Scythian Ares") who was only depicted in the form of a sword lain atop a pile of sticks. This symbol itself forms the depiction of the god. This is supported by a practice of successor peoples, the **Alans** and **Ossetians**, who would stab a sword into the earth and worship that, itself, as their god of war. Similarly, according to Tacitus, the **Germanic** peoples *"do not consider it consistent with the grandeur of celestial beings to confine the gods within walls, or to liken them to the form of any human countenance. They consecrate woods and groves, and they apply the names of deities to the abstraction which they see only in spiritual worship"*. However, there have been finds from German sites where gods are apparently depicted in human-like form, which indicates that Tacitus' observations were not universal.

7.5 Music

The history of music is older than humanity itself. Animals such as birds, whales and dolphins have been found to both respond to, and produce, sounds that are considered pleasing to their ears. With that said, it is no surprise that throughout human history, people have sought similarly appealing sounds to provoke a variety of emotional reactions. In addition to this use, music also served as a medium for oral tradition and storytelling. This was because music made memorization easier. For this reason, musicians often possessed an important role in society, alongside poets and lawspeakers. The emotional affect of music also made it an important tool for affecting large groups of people, whether worshipers in prayer or warriors before battle.

One particular quirk of discussing musical history is that, without readable musical notation, modern scholars often have an incomplete idea of what ancient music sounded like. The oldest "translated" song - which is to say, a song with musical notation that can be understood by people today - is the *Seikilos Epitaph*, a 2nd century **Greek** funeral song. However, we do have information about the instruments ancient peoples used, both through their accounts and through archaeological findings. We also have an understanding of the role it played through descriptions of it in contemporary writing.

Percussion instruments make sound by striking a surface, whether solid or membranous (i.e. stretched skin). The sound of the instrument depends on the surface hit, as well as other factors that can be controlled by the musician. This category includes drums, rattles, cymbals, tambourines and bells. It also includes "human percussion" such as clapping or body-slapping, which are naturally the oldest forms of percussion alongside striking random objects. Those forms of percussion are practiced even by animals, such as primates. Among macaque monkeys, drumming is a practice done only by the largest and most powerful monkeys, suggesting it has a social aspect of dominance.

Drums originate in **Egypt** and **China**. Old Chinese drums consisted of clay vessels with alligator skin stretched over their tops. Other drums were made with copper or wood, with other animal skins used for their percussive membrane. Drums could be also made entirely out of metal, such as all-bronze drums found from ancient **Vietnam**. A specific subtype of drum is the *hourglass drum*, which had a thin center. The outer rims of the drum surfaces would be held together with lace stretched between the two surfaces. These laces could be manipulated during a performance to make different sounds. Such drums were found in **India**, **Korea**, **Japan** and **West Africa**. In addition to their artistic uses, drums could also be used for communication, military organization, and intimidation. In some cases, the shields of soldiers or warriors would be used as a makeshift drum, such as the cowhide shields of the **Zulu** people.

Rattles are a common early instrument. They are made from hollow gourds or wood, which are then filled with beans, pebbles or other small objects in order to make noise when shaken. Examples include the *maraca*, originating amongst aboriginal peoples of **Brazil**, the *rainstick* of the Patagonian **Mapuche** people, the *hosho* of Zimbabwe's **Shona** people, and the **Egyptian** *sistrum*.

Tambourines are a combination of a small hand-held drum with small cymbals or bells attached to the frame. Most are played as both a drum and a rattling instrument. Examples include the **Hebrew** *timbrel,* central Asian *dayereh* and **Iranian** *daf.* The timbrel dates back to the Old Testament, which indicates that it was taken from the **Egyptians**. The daf has a later origin, coming from the Iranian Sassanid dynasty (224-651 CE).

Wind instruments make noise when air passes through them, most commonly from human breath. This category includes horns, flutes, and pipes.

Horns were originally literal animal horns, hollowed out and opened up for use as an instrument. The **Hebrew** *shofar* is an example that is still in use for modern religious rituals. Shells could also be used in a similar way, such as the **Indian** *shankha*. An alternative was the birch trumpet, or *neverlur*, used in ancient **Scandinavia**, which was made of lightweight wood and bark. A variation of this, the *lur*, was one of the first metal horns, dating back to the 10th century BCE. Most variations on the basic metal horn model were centered around different shapes or designs, such as the semi-spiral **Roman** *buccina* and *cornu*. It was not until more complex metallurgy became possible (in 18th century Europe) that more complex instruments such as trumpets and French horns became possible. Horns in general were used for signals and warnings, because they were easy to use and produced a loud, distinct sound.

Flutes and *pipes* both consist of a frame that is hollow and open, with two main holes - one for the musician to breathe into, and the other for air to exit from. Other holes are sometimes along the frame to affect the sound of the instrument. The fingers are used to cover these holes while playing in order to modulate the note. An alternative is the "Pan flute" model, which has pipes of different length held together with twine or rope. Each pipe produces a different note, so the musician plays by blowing into the desired pipe. Most pipes are made from wood, reeds or bamboo. The oldest were carved from bone and exist in both the hole-based and Pan models. Hardened clay was sometimes used as well. Pipes are common in every part of the world. Some examples include the *quray* of the Turkic **Bakshir** people, the *digiredoo* of the aboriginal **Australians**, and the **Laotian** *wot*, which is a circular version of the Pan flute model.

Bagpipes are a variation on the standard pipe model where an array of pipes are connected to an airtight bag usually made of animal skin. The oldest model is the **Greek** *askaulos*, although the exact model and nature of it is debated. The **Scottish** bagpipe, arguably the most famous, originates from the 17th century CE, and the **Turkmen** bagpipe, which influenced the Middle Eastern tradition, dates from the 19th. Text-based evidence for Scottish "warpipes" dates back to the 1400s, although this is less concrete than the evidence that came later.

An unusual "wind" instrument is the *bullroarer*, which consists of a weighted slat of wood attached to a long string. The slat is swung in a large circle around the musician's head, and as air passes through it, a loud sound is generated. Bullroarers date back to around 17000 BCE, and were commonly used by **Australian** aborigines for long-distance communication. Other examples come from the **Dogon** of Mali, the **Maori**, the **Greeks**, the **Scandinavians** and the **Picts**.

String instruments generate sound by plucking or bowing a stretched "string" made of animal intestine or, sometimes, silk. These strings are mounted on a frame usually made of wood, and sometimes of metal. There are three main types of string instrument, separated by construction type.

Harp-type instruments have a hollow frame, with the strings stretched between it. A harp-style instrument, the *lyre*, is the oldest known string instrument. The oldest surviving lyre dates back to the 25th century BCE, in the **Mesopotamian** city of Ur. Others include the **Iranian** *chang*, the **Chinese** *konghou* (and **Korean** *gonghu*), and the *yazh* of southern **India**.

Lute-type instruments have a base and a neck, with the strings stretched across their surface. Its sub-categories include the guitar, violin, and fiddle. Specific examples include the **Iranian** *barbat* and *tanbur*, the **Japanese** *biwa*, the **Greek** *pandura*, and the **Hausa** *goje*.

Zither-type instruments stretch the strings across a solid surface, similar to a lute-type but without the base-and-neck design. The oldest zither is the **Chinese** *guqin*, which dates back to the 5th century BCE. Most ancient zithers originate from Asia, including the **Indonesian** *celempung*, the **Mongolian** *yatga*, and the **Japanese** *koto*, which uses silk strings.

The final "instrument" mentioned here is the voice. Like every other form of human-based music, singing is as old as humanity. However, there are several specialized versions of it in different cultures.

James Shea

Chanting is a common form of singing used for religious rituals. Chants often base themselves on a relatively simple, slow rhythm, with religious texts (such as Christian *psalms* or Buddhist *mantras*) used as lyrics. Chants vary in complexity, from simple chants designed for large groups or congregations to more complex ones designed for a smaller group of trained singers.

In early medieval Europe, most music (including chanting) was *monophonic,* meaning that songs had only a single melody rather than multiple overlapping ones. Songs of this type were designed for a single singer, and when done by multiple singers they were all supposed to hit the same notes. This restriction was intentionally engineered by the church; in 1324 CE, Pope John XXII issued a statement called *Docta Sanctorum Patrum* which expressly condemned polyphonic songs as undignified and "indecent" because of their increased emotional effect. However, the later Pope Clement VI (1342-1352) did not agree and encouraged it. One of the oldest European polyphonic pieces is the "Summer Canon", an **English** song designed with six distinct melodies, written in the mid-13th century.

"Throat-singing" is practiced by many central Asian and northeast Asian cultures, such as the **Mongolians**, the **Tibetans**, the **Tuvans**, the **Altai**, the **Inuit** and the **Ainu**. Throat-singing involves manipulating vocal resonance to produce a low, droning pitch in addition to additional simultaneous pitches.

Flyting was a practice among the **Norse** and **Anglo-Saxon** peoples dating back to the 5th century CE. It was, in essence, a contest of boasts or insults conducted in verse. These contests were done among large groups of onlookers, who would decide the winner by popular outcry. Comparable "verbal combat" practices exist in some other cultures, such as the **Nigerian** "*Ikocha Nkocha*". Historian Elijah Wald connects that practice to the modern African-American practice of "The Dozens", a similar game of verbal jabs and insults.

In **China**, *kouji* is a vocal mimicry practice that dates back to (at least) the Tang dynasty, although some evidence suggests it may be older.

163

Kouji is the art of vocal mimicry, used to accentuate storytelling or as a form of entertainment in its own right. Birds and other animals are a common subject for mimicry, but complex sounds such as the sounds of battle or a busy marketplace were often helpful for storytelling purposes. Kouji is related to the wider concept of "vocal percussion", using the voice to imitate instruments. Most established methods of vocal percussion come from relatively recent history, but some are older - such as the *juba* dance of **West Africa** or the *konnakol* of the **Tamil** people. More recent examples include scatting and beatboxing, both deriving from African-American communities.

VIII. WARFARE & MILITARISM

For all but a few societies, warfare is a fact of life. War creates group unity against targeted outsiders, it allows individuals a chance to display masculine values, and it allows for the acquisition of land and resources. Even if a society itself eschews militancy, its neighbors probably don't. Warfare is politics, it is self defense, and it is power in identity.

8.1 Martial Attitude

Societies generally have three overarching attitudes towards violence. The first is built around combat and war, where violence is practiced by many members and is seen as a moral good on its own. The second is where war is treated as a normal political tool, but is not as well-regarded and is carried out by specific segments of society. The third is where violence is rejected entirely, although in some cases it may be acceptable as a tool of self-preservation. These attitudes are characterized as "aggressive", "mixed" and "pacifistic".

Aggressive societies, or warrior cultures, are built around values of bravery and strength first and foremost. Concerns such as smithing and farming are tolerated only as support to martial endeavors. One of those most famous warrior cultures is that of the **Spartans**, a society in **Greece** that subjected all its male citizens to harsh training from an early age. As mentioned earlier, the Spartans relied on slaves (*helots*) to handle structural needs, while true Spartans concerned themselves only with masculine pursuits. The Spartans are relatively unique among warrior peoples, in that their entire "proper" society was organized around violence. Other aggressive cultures, such as the **Maori**, **Germanic** peoples, **Jivaro**, and **Yanomami**, balance their aggression with aspects of more civilian life. The Spartans were unique because they delegated every non-military role to the helot class. On the whole, aggressive societies generally engage in war even when it is not politically necessary. This is called "endemic warfare" and is covered later in this chapter. Warfare of this type was seen as a way to show masculine virtues and ties into the idea of violence being its own good.

Mixed societies represented the average or the norm. Mixed societies generally had a warrior "element" in their culture, but it did not permeate the culture as a whole. For example, medieval **Europe** was built around a tripartite social order - a division between *oratores* (those who pray), *bellatores* (those who fight), and *laboratores* (those who work). In such a system, combat was not pervasive throughout society, but was intentionally limited to this warrior subculture. These subcultures also frequently had an ideological code meant to broaden their interests and values, such as the European code of chivalry, or the Arabic *furusiyya*. This added depth to their role and gave them societal functions besides mere combat.

Pacifistic societies are based on high empathy and respect for human life. In many cases, pacifism is religiously motivated, based on a perception of purity and souls that goes beyond the physical plane. In other cases, a society existed in a protected region where military conflict was simply unnecessary. Pacifist societies avoided conflict wherever possible, but violence in self-defense was sometimes justified. Because pacifistic societies are comparatively rare, detailed examples will be provided.

The Polynesian **Moriori** people lived by a code called "Nunuku's Law", which forbade killing a human for any reason, and especially cannibalism. Aggression was handled by ritualistic, non-lethal fighting. The reason for this is thought to be the limited resources in their home, Rekohu (now the Chatham Islands). War consumes resources and could have created an imbalance that would have doomed their society - similar to what may have happened to the inhabitants of Easter Island.

However, the Moriori were eventually invaded by their far more aggressive cousins, the warlike **Maori**. While there was dissent in the Moriori leadership, it was ultimately decided that they must stand by their pacifistic principles. The Moriori attempted to flee and hide, but it did not avail them. The Maori hunted them down and dragged them from their hiding places. 10% of them were killed, painfully and slowly, and their bodies were cannibalized. The survivors were all enslaved, banned from speaking their native language and forced to defile their holy places.

The **Hopi** people of the American southwest are known in their language as "the peaceful peoples" (*Hopituh Shi-nu-mu*).Their name can also be translated as "one who follows the Hopi way", which is the way of peace and reverence for all things. The origins of this philosophy are difficult to ascertain. The Hopi were occasionally forced to fight for their own survival, notably against the **Navajo** people, who were pushed into their territory by American settlements and reservations.

Christianity produced several pacifistic branches due to Christ's dogma of "turning the other cheek". However, these branches were always a minority, and were often persecuted by the Catholic majority. The **Cathar** movement, for example, rejected all killing (except, occasionally, for fish). They also disliked sex, or more specifically reproduction, and granted equal opportunities to women in almost every field. These beliefs were founded in their theological view of the world. Specifically, the physical world was considered evil, and pure living was necessary to escape it. The Catholic Church attempted to peacefully reconcile the Cathars for many years, until 1207, when a papal legate was murdered on his way back from their holdings in Southern France. With this pretext, the Pope launched the Albigensian Crusade. Unlike the Moriori, the Cathars often *did* fight back (although many towns surrendered without violence). However, they were ultimately annihilated in a brutal campaign that many historians now recognize as a genocide - including the scholar who invented the term. The Crusade was also the origin of the phrase *"Caedite eos. Novit enim Dominus qui sunt eius"* (Kill them all, God will know his own).

Another pacifistic Christian sect was the 19th century **Shaker** movement. Like the Cathars, the Shakers were communal, pacifistic, celibate and gender-egalitarian. Unlike the Cathars, they were lucky enough to live in an area without external persecution. During the Civil War, President Lincoln specifically exempted Shakers from military service. However, due to their celibacy, Shaker communities were reliant entirely on outside converts, and their economic model simply couldn't keep up with the outside world. Their failing economy (and thus quality of life) scared away potential converts and eventually the Shakers dwindled to a tiny number of communities.

The **Religious Society of Friends**, or **Quakers**, were another group of Pacifist Christians. They were not as extreme as the Cathars or Shakers, but did hold many beliefs of their own, such as "plain dress" (i.e. only unadorned clothing), opposition to slavery, and opposition to alcohol. The Quakers were more financially successful than the Shakers due to their more open belief system, and thus continue to prosper even today.

Moving away from Christendom, two historical groups in India were notable for their abstention from violence. The first of these is the **Harappan Civilization**, also known as the **Indus Valley Civilization**. The Harappan language is currently not understood (due to the lack of a transitory "Rosetta Stone" that could be used to translate it), but based on artifacts and findings, archaeologists generally see the Harappans as an egalitarian and peaceful society. The former claim is based on the equality of houses found in their cities. The latter was determined by the fact that there are no signs of mass warfare, including ash layers (i.e. the city being burned down), weapon caches, or even depictions of warfare in their artwork.

The other notable example from India is the *Jainist* religion. Among its other values, Jainism promotes the idea of Ahimsa, or supreme non-violence. This is non-violence that, like Catharism, is extended to all living things, although the Jainists take it even further. Jainists do not intentionally kill insects, and even root vegetables are considered taboo by the more devout (the reason being that pulling up a root vegetable damages tiny organisms under the earth). Even food taken in "good" ways, such as dairy products or fruits, are treated respectfully, and are only eaten as necessary. Unlike the Moriori people, Jainists see self-defense as a necessity, albeit an unpleasant one. They also draw a distinction between accidental killing and knowing/intentional killing.

8.2 Intensity of Warfare

When discussing "war", it is first necessary to discuss what *kind* of war is being discussed. Talking about different levels of war is as important as talking about the difference between a bar-room brawl and a deliberate murder. Almost every culture had rules, or at least customs, for war, and those rules would have been different if one was fighting one's neighbor or if one was fighting a foreign invader.

The lowest level of warfare is endemic war. Endemic warfare is an ongoing, low-level form of combat that is often found between tribal groups. In endemic warfare, neither conquest nor extermination are the goal. Rather, it is a form of "violent sport". Earlier I talked about the benefits that war brings to traditional communities - it unites the group against outsiders, it allows individuals a chance to develop and display masculine values, etc. The purpose of endemic warfare is to reap those benefits without the risk of major upheaval. In short, it is a highly ritualized form of combat focused on bravery and ceremony, rather than a pragmatically-waged war of conquest. However, it is important to note that blood feuds may develop as the result of events during endemic warfare, which raise the stakes dramatically.

One example of endemic warfare are the *flower wars* conducted by the **Aztec** civilization. Aztec culture placed a great deal of importance on frequent human sacrifice. Captives obtained during wars of conquest were often used to fulfill these requirements. Indeed, during these "serious" wars, Aztec warriors fought intentionally to wound for the sake of obtaining captives, rather than killing enemies outright. The "flower wars" took this a step further; they were arranged, organized battles designed *solely* for the taking of sacrifices, with different rules and expectations compared to a serious war. For example, ranged weapons were not commonly used in flower wars, and the number of combatants was pre-arranged beforehand in order to be equal. These wars were so important that the Aztecs (according to Moctezuma II) let many of its neighbors exist independently solely so they could participate in these ritualized flower wars. These neighbors participated because the alternative was full-on conquest or extermination.

Similar to the flower wars, the indigenous people of the American Northeast (including the **Mohicans**, **Susquehannock** and **Haudosaunee**) conducted *mourning wars.* Mourning wars were connected to blood feuds or debts; attacks would be carried out in retaliation for earlier attacks, which would then be the impetus for further revenge afterwards. These wars were conducted for societal reasons moreso than for tactical ones; the goal was not to destroy the enemy, but simply to avenge debts and earn warrior accolades. Captives would also be taken during mourning wars, and these captives would either be sacrificed (similar to flower wars) or adopted into their captor clan. In this way, the population could be maintained, with the captives replacing lost members of the tribe. These captives often gave up their old ways and assimilated fully into their new tribe. The Haudosaunee in particular gained in size and power due to their military successes and captive adoption, which gave them a large and diverse population.

Another example of endemic warfare is the *cattle raid*, examples of which can be found from **Ireland** to **India** to **Africa**. Cattle were seen by many civilizations as a key form of wealth, as they produced many necessary items (milk, meat, leather, etc.) of benefit to their owners. Cattle raids thus had a large economic impetus behind them, but were markedly different than wars of conquest. In Ireland especially, the cattle raid (or "Tain Bo") formed the basis for many mythological stories. The most famous of these is the "Tain Bo Cuailnge", or the "Cattle Raid of Cooley", which features the hero Cu Chulainn. In **North Africa**, raiding was known as *ghazw*, and the warriors who participated in it were known as *ghazi*. When carried out against neighbors, it was a form of endemic warfare. However, it could also be a form of total war carried out against non-Muslims; this form of raiding was later adopted by Christian **Iberians**, who called it *razzia*.

The **Bantu** people of southern Africa engaged in ritualized warfare, often with agreed-upon conditions and meeting points. Casualties were generally low, since neither side really wanted to die, and ransoming or extortion were more common. The end results were similarly small, with no major conquests or exterminations. In contrast to this, by the 19th century their wars had become more serious and consequential. Some historians place the responsibility for this change on Shaka, leader of the Zulu Kingdom, who reorganized his tribe's military and made it a far more effective and pragmatic fighting force. However, one of Shaka's early battles was against a larger opponent - the Ndwandwe people under King Zwide. Furthermore, oral tradition suggests that Zwide's goal was the extermination of the Zulu people, which goes against the earlier endemic model. While Shaka's contributions to military tactics and logistics are undeniable, the numbers and tone of this campaign suggest that the shift to a larger, more serious type of warfare had already happened.

The next level of warfare is the limited war. This is a war constrained by legal precedent, or *casus belli*. Such wars are fought between powers that, for one reason or another, have binding agreements and relationships in place that affect the intensity of their conflict. These ties may be familial in nature (shared culture or identity) or it may simply be a balance of power situation - an agreed-upon set of limitations that exist for the common good. In comparison to endemic warfare, the stakes are higher. Large parcels of land or wealth may change hands during such conflict. However, the scale is generally smaller when compared to a total war; since such ventures are traditionally grabs for power, it does not make sense to uproot the entire country to deal with it.

One common feature of limited wars is the idea of *ransom*. Ransom is the capturing and releasing of prisoners in exchange for payment. In many cases only noble soldiers are subject to ransom. Ransom was common in the wars of medieval **Europe**, but also in **Southeast Asia**, in *Islamic* nations, and others. In Europe, the practice of ransom led to visible displays of individual heraldry - to show one's status and incite enemies to attempt to capture, rather than kill, the wearer. This was reversed in the **English** *War of the Roses*, where the stakes involved led to many nobles being killed immediately for treason rather than being captured, while common soldiers were let go. Islam had many rules about how to humanely deal with prisoners of war; according to some sources, it was possible for a literate individual to earn their freedom by teaching a set number of Muslims to read and write. However, the exact rules in Islam for the treatment of prisoners are widely disputed.

The *Hundred Years' War* is an example of a war built upon legal precedent. Specifically, Edward III of **England** had a claim to the throne of **France** through his mother's line. However, in the years between her birth and the time of that claim being made, France had established Salic law. This denied inheritance through the female line, among other things. Nonetheless, Edward III pressed his claim, primarily motivated by French interference in his wars against Scotland. Notably, the English did target civilians intentionally (as opposed to them being targets of opportunity), but this actually exists for a "limited war" reason. It was a practice known as *chevauchee*, and its purpose was actually to encourage the victimized towns to reject the French crown. In short, it was making the case that the French king was too incompetent to protect his people, and that the English king (who was actually *doing* the raiding) was more qualified. Even though the violence targeted civilians, it did so in order to lend support and credibility for Edward III's claim to the throne, thus making it a component of the legalistic limited war.

Regarding the earlier point about a smaller amount of soldiers, the Hundred Years' War gives us some good figures to work with. At the battle of *Crecy* in 1346, the English army numbered around 10,000 troops (give or take a thousand). In comparison with that figure, the total population of England at the time was around 3 million. This was certainly a "war", but only .3% of the population was actually involved. For the rest of the country, life continued as usual. The French army was larger, but proportionally matched the overall French population. French civilians only became involved as targets of raiding and looting by the English forces.

Another such war involving the English crown is the war of succession following the death of Edward the Confessor, also known as the

Norman Invasion of England. This war involved King Harold II of
England, King Harald III of **Norway**, and Duke William II of
Normandy. Each had a claim to the throne due to the lack of a direct
successor on Edward's part. Harold of England had been elected by the
Witenagemot, a council of nobles that traditionally advised the king,
and thus was the popular candidate among the Anglo-Saxon nobility.
Harald of Norway based his claim on an earlier agreement between
King Magnus of Norway and King Canute III of England and
Denmark, Edward's immediate predecessor. Finally, William based
his claim on the statement that Edward himself had promised the throne
to him, and in addition he had Papal support for his invasion (thus
legitimizing it in the eyes of Christendom).

Each of these kings attempted to hold the English crown, and when
William won it created massive cultural changes throughout the
country. Nonetheless, it was still fighting on a relatively small scale,
with numbers similar to those of Crecy. Even though it was a war that
drastically affected the lives of the common folk, it was still considered
an affair of noblemen and their immediate subordinates.

The *Kabinettskriege* (cabinet wars) of the 1700s may be the purest
example of the "limited war" concept. These wars were fought by
small, highly controlled state armies who rigorously followed the laws
and regulations of war at the time. Following a period of religious
violence, the cabinet wars cut down on looting and violence against
civilians, instead focusing much more on agreed-upon military goals
and targets. War was fought for specific agreed-upon reasons (*jus ad
bellum*) and in specific agreed-upon ways (*jus in bello*).

During **China**'s *Shang* and *Zhou* dynasties, war had a more "chivalric"
aspect than it did in later years. It was reported in some cases that one
country would not invade another if they were in mourning for the
death of their ruler, and they would make sure that a noble bloodline
was never fully wiped out so someone would exist to pay homage to
their ancestors. In one incident, Xiang, the ruler of the state of Song,
refused to press a tactical advantage (an ambush on a river crossing)
because he thought it would be unfair. In the battle that followed,

Xiang was wounded and his forces were badly routed. The era that followed was the Warring States period, which was marked by much more pragmatic warmaking.

Following the limited war is the total war. A total war is a war without major restrictions, where all members of a given society are considered valid targets, whether or not they are combatants. Total wars are carried out against enemies who do not carry the legal or cultural associations necessary to justify less-intense warfare. For example, limited warfare existed in medieval Europe because of a distaste for violence against fellow Catholics (although exceptions always existed). When wars were carried out against pagans or heretics or infidels, they took on a markedly different tone. Sometimes, limited wars would turn into total wars based on the intensity of the rivalries involved; this was the case with the **Greek** Peloponnesian War between Athens and Sparta.

In contrast with the numbers given for limited wars, total wars sometimes include the idea of *levee en masse*, or mass conscription. The term itself came from the **French** *Revolutionary Wars*, where citizens were called up in unheard-of numbers to defend the fledgling republic from its aristocratic enemies. While the idea was largely unpopular, and many conscripts deserted, its military effectiveness created a shift towards such massive armies, culminating in millions-vs-millions conflicts such as the *First World War*.

In **Japan**, the *Onin War* of 1467 to 1477 represented a shift from a ritualized limited war to a crueler, more dangerous total war. Japanese wars of earlier periods were fought between noble houses, and only involved nobles and their immediate retainers. The idea of involving peasants was not accepted, since combat itself was honor-bound in nature. However, the Onin War was a gruesome urban conflict fought almost entirely in the streets of the capital, Kyoto. It involved roughly 160,000 soldiers, who entrenched themselves with fortifications and barricades in various parts of the city. Kyoto itself was mostly destroyed in the conflict, and displaced townsfolk were actually recruited into the war with promises of loot and food. These peasants were considered unreliable due to their lack of loyalty and motivation, but their numbers and desperation compelled lordly commanders to press them into service. This resulted in two major shifts in Japanese society. It marked the first use of *ashigaru*, or common soldiers employed by feudal lords. It also predicated the rise of the *ikko ikki*, rebel peasant groups battling the feudal system itself. Both concepts would become more organized and prominent in later years.

A potential component of a total war is the idea of communal violence. Communal violence is essentially a form of violence that involves people at every layer of society. Endemic warfare can build up to this level as blood-feuding and ethnic differences become the impetus for true tension. It is this sort of feuding that led to the *Yugoslav Wars*, in which brutal ethnic cleansing was carried out by militants at all levels of society, not just official government soldiers. Religion is a similarly powerful factor; conflicts between Catholics and Protestants in Europe included everything from combat between noble armies to riots in the streets of major cities, such as the *1562 Toulouse Riots*.

Even "noble" wars involving Catholic & Protestant identities tended to have vicious layers of communal violence, such as the *Thirty Years' War*. That conflict began as the result of a **German** Emperor trying to impose Catholicism on all of his people, which resulted in rebellions, which themselves resulted in foreign intervention on either the Catholic or Protestant side. The divisive nature of the conflict, along with the wide use of mercenaries, resulted in a large number of looted villages and towns, burned crops, and terrorized civilians. The war caused famine and disease on a massive scale, and civilian populations were reduced dramatically. In many German regions the population drop was between 25% and 40%; in others, such as Württemberg, saw losses as high as 75%. The horrors and damage of the Thirty Years' War were a key component for the development of the "cabinet wars" discussed in the previous section. Many of the laws of war that defined the Kabinettskriege era were written into the Treaty of Westphalia, which ended the Thirty Years' War.

In much later years, the concept of "national identity" gained increasing prominence and had a similar polarizing effect to earlier religious identity. In the 19th century, nationalism became a popular concept, influenced by many philosophies and events of the day. One example of this is the rise of nationalism in the **Ottoman Empire**. In short, the Ottomans ruled over southeastern Europe, an area which included many different peoples - **Arabs**, **Greeks**, **Albanians**, **Serbs**, **Kosovars**, **Bulgarians**, on and on. The Ottoman Empire allowed these people a certain amount of independence and did not attempt to culturally assimilate them in the way that the Romans had "Romanized" the provinces they conquered. Before the rise of nationalism, this was a convenient, low-effort arrangement where vassal states were relatively self-managing. When ethnic identity became more important, these various peoples chafed at foreign rule, and a series of independence revolts (or "*National Awakenings*") ensued. These revolts represent a shift from a relatively "limited war" scenario to full-on communal violence against perceived Ottoman oppression. In short, national identity militarized the people as a whole.

The relationship between the **Pawnee** and **Sioux** peoples of the American Great Plains is an example of a communal war that arose out of an endemic war. All members of the opposing tribe were considered fair game. Non-combatants were considered just as valuable targets as warriors, under the justification that taking a scalp from a non-combatant meant that the warrior had infiltrated deep into enemy territory to obtain it. In the *Massacre Canyon Battle*, a group of 1000 Sioux fell upon 750 Pawnee (half men, the rest women and children) heading for their summer hunting grounds. According to reports from survivors (both Pawnee and American agents with them), the Sioux brutalized Pawnee women and children. According to one account, detailed in the Chicago Tribute (Aug. 30, 1873), the Sioux "took the children by the heels and beat their brains out on the ground". These sorts of actions are founded in ongoing contempt and dehumanization, and transcend "war" as a mere political concept.

8.3 Nature of Soldiery

The combatants involved in a given conflict will generally correlate with the type of conflict it is. As mentioned, wars can range from a constrained affair featuring only elites to a society-wide ideological struggle. However, this segment deals with who is *generally* a soldier in a given society, i.e. who is given training, who is expected to fight and how they are equipped. There are roughly three types of combatants, sorted by their motivations, and one notable peculiarity.

<u>Soldiers who fight for group loyalty</u> are the oldest type of combatants, as their loyalty came from clan or tribal ties. This is an egalitarian sort of soldier, motivated not by loyalty to a superior, but to a community. As cultural values developed throughout history, this category expanded to include those driven by religious motivation or ideological purpose (such as peasant rebellions). Soldiers in this category may be fulfilling an obligation, but ultimately their loyalty is to a group or idea, rather than being based on subservience to a position.

<u>Soldiers who fight for pay</u> come in two subgroups. The first of these are *retainers*, who are employed long-term and are often equipped and trained by their employer. The second are *mercenaries*, who are hired temporarily and thus have a different relationship with their employer than more permanent soldiers do. In many cultures, an army would consist of a small core of professionals and a larger group of part-time levied soldiers. Some cultures were able to recruit large groups of professional soldiers to serve as their primary fighting force; this is called a *standing army*. In other cases, paid units (especially *foreign* paid units) were used as a bodyguard by unpopular rulers, since they lacked any local loyalties or ties. One example of this was the *Varangian Guard* of the **Byzantine Empire**, which was staffed by **Norsemen** and **Anglo-Saxons**.

<u>Soldiers who fight for obligations</u> also come in two subgroups: upper-class and lower-class. *Upper-class* obliged soldiers are given tracts of land known as *fiefs* to manage. These fiefs generate money for the obliged soldier, and they are required to use some of that money to

equip themselves and a number of retainers. They are responsible for their own training, as well. In times of war, they are called to their liege's banner to support their military campaign. In contrast, *lower-class* obliged soldiers are common folk required by law to act as soldiers for their ruler's army. In some cases, such as **England**, only higher-ranking common folk (i.e. yeoman farmers) were required to muster, in exchange for certain privileges. In other cases, such as early **Chinese** history, general conscription was carried out in massive numbers. Levies carry the particular issue that they are often required to be both soldiers *and* farmers, and thus can only be used for short periods of time before they must be returned to tend their fields.

The final type of soldier to be discussed is the slave-soldier. Slaves forced to fight for their masters (or who were offered their freedom in exchange for service) were not that uncommon, and generally provided mediocre service - not surprising given their lack of motivation. However, what we're talking about is professional, career-driven "slave-soldiers". This is an institution found primarily in Muslim nations. The most common example is that of the *mamluks*, who were found from **Egypt** to **Turkey** to **India**. The slaves were taken from non-Muslim populations, as it was considered improper for a Muslim to enslave another Muslim. The slaves were then given severe and austere military training. Because of their lack of family ties or political connections they were considered to be ideal soldiers. Once they joined military service, their lives were pleasant, even luxurious, despite their unfree status. Many "slave-soldiers" rose to high status in society (including command and land-owning), even as they were bound to their noble owners. This is not to say the system was "perfect", as there were several major revolts throughout history led by the slave-soldier class.

In ancient **Mesopotamia**, evidence exists that points to both levies and a core professional army. Notably, it would be the *oldest* professional army in known history. The *Instructions of Shupparak*, a set of tablets used as a guide for rulership, detailed the practice of having 600 to 700 paid professional soldiers, whose equipment and supplies would be provided by the state. These soldiers would fight in the first known shield-wall or phalanx, which required more discipline and training than other tactics of the time.

The disparate kingdoms of **China** originally used a small aristocratic core supplemented by massive levies of barely-trained, poorly-equipped peasantry. In these early *Shang* and *Zhou* dynasties, warfare was primarily the domain of the chariot-mounted nobility, with the peasantry as a barely-considered sideshow. Eventually the system broke down, and the Warring States period that followed was marked by more organized and professional armies led by officers chosen by merit. The majority of soldiers were still obtained through mass conscription, but they were given superior training and gear, and combat was more tactical in nature. The *Han* dynasty focused more on professional soldiers with a supplementary unit of drafted farmers, usually for supply or building purposes. The *Wei* dynasty created the concept of *buqu*, which made military positions hereditary. A soldier with a buqu position would fight for a lord, and on his death a male relative would take that position. Buqu families had special restrictions to ensure a constant fighting force, one of which was that buqu families were required to intermarry rather than marrying outside the class.

The **Greek** city-states were defined largely by their citizen armies. As discussed earlier, "citizen" had an important meaning in Greece, containing both privileges and obligation. When the city-state went to war, a citizen was required to equip themselves according to their rank and ability and go on campaign. The poorest would be used as rowers or as skirmishers, the middle class would form the heavy *hoplite* units, and the richest would serve as cavalry. The lower ranks would also serve as attendants to those above them when not in battle. Their service could be either based on obligation (under a tyrant) or group loyalty (in a democracy). This was the difference between being compelled by an authority figure, and cooperation for an agreed-upon purpose.

The **Roman Empire** had two major phases based on a set of decrees called the Marian Reforms (107 BC). Prior to the reforms, the Roman army was similar to the Greek model, but available only to the upper classes. The Marian Reforms changed the army at its very core. Firstly, it became a true *standing army*, with positions available to any citizen willing and able. These citizens were paid, trained, and equipped by the state, and those who survived to retirement were given a generous pension and land grant. They were also full-time professional soldiers, rather than part-time citizen soldiers. In this way, the army became an efficient, organized machine that offered a reliable way of advancement for poor citizens. On the other hand, the new legions were frequently used as political tools by their commanding generals, and their loyalty could often be bought and sold independent of any imperial obligations. The core legions were supplemented by *auxiliaries*, conquered non-Roman provincial subjects hired with regular pay and the promise of citizenship. Auxiliaries were chosen based on their special skills, such as Cretan archers, Balearic slingers, and Gallic cavalry. This offered a breadth of tactical options to the Roman military, as well as aiding in the spread of Roman culture and values.

The **Anglo-Saxons** had three military layers: the land-holding *thegns*, the retainer *huscarls*, and the levied *fyrd*. When Harold Godwinson was preparing for the invasion of William of Normandy, the time limits on his fyrd were a major tactical issue for him. Harold spent the summer of 1066 with his armies on England's southern coast, but the fyrd could not be held for harvesting season and had to be dismissed in September. Later that month, the King of Norway invaded, forcing Harold to fight him off at the Battle of Stamford Bridge with only his huscarls and thegns.

The **Scandinavians** shared the same word "*huscarl*" as the Anglo-Saxons, but instead of a fyrd, they had a fleet-levy called the *leidang*. This had both offensive and defensive purposes. All free men were obliged to take part in the leidang, and communities were organized around it (each district was obliged to provide one ship and crew). While maintaining the ship & crew was mandatory, the full leidang was rarely called up. However, there would be many volunteers for raids, since raids held the opportunity for looting.

The **Rus** people had a concept, *druzhina*, wherein a ruler's advisors (*boyars*) would offer their sons as soldiers and bodyguards. Both Boyars and their sons were voluntarily associated with a given ruler, and were generally free to leave when they pleased. The ruler would earn the loyalty of their boyars by sharing taxes and loot with them. Eventually, some boyars were granted land and titles, which created a system similar to feudalism on top of the existing druzhina agreement.

In **India**, the *kshatriya* caste fulfilled the warrior role. India is far from monolithic, and there are many divergent models and castes based on local systems. For this reason we will focus on one text in particular: the *Arthashastra*, an Indian book of statecraft and governance written some time in the 3rd century BCE. According to the Arthashastra, kshatriya could be either landed & hereditary (*maula*) or merely hired retainers (*bhrta*). The normal ranks of Indian armies came from trade guild levies (i.e. skilled craftsmen, rather than conscripted peasants). These levies were called *sreni-balam*; when not on campaign, they served as guards for their home cities. Indian rulers would also hire forest tribes, or *atavi-balam*, with promises of plunder.

In the **Frankish Empire**, Charlemagne rewarded his elite cavalry units with benefices, a.k.a. fiefs. The impetus for this was the conquests Charlemagne had been carrying out; handing out land to warriors simultaneously rewarded the warrior for their service, while also guaranteeing an armed, trained presence to guard the land in question. Under Charles the Bald, these positions were made hereditary, and the class itself became more distinct. This is what eventually became *knighthood*, and formed the basis for military organization in much of feudal Europe. A similar concept developed much earlier, in **Armenia**, with the *azats*. When Franks met Armenians during the Crusades, the similarity of the two institutions was noted by the nobleman Smbat Sparapet.

In **Japan**, the *samurai* began as members of noble families tasked by the emperor to deal with rebellions and indigenous peoples. As they came to ignore the authority of the Emperor, these clans became powerful political players in their own right. Combat between these noble families was highly ritualized, with a focus on mounted archery and individual duals. During the tumultuous Sengoku period, commoners joined the fighting, starting as standing-army *ashigaru* but potentially earning their way to hereditary positions and becoming samurai themselves. This pragmatic, merit-based approach soon ended after the Shogun Toyotomi Hideyoshi (himself a former commoner) solidified the class system as a formal caste arrangement, preventing further social mobility.

In **Korea**, specifically the Kingdom of Silla, there was a societal layer of warriors called *hwarang*, or "flowering knights". They were professional warriors with a code of chivalry and good conduct, armed with sword, bow, and javelin. However, one notable difference between the hwarang and other similar warrior-castes is that the hwarang were also meant to represent an ideal of beauty and grace as well as martial and moral ideals. They became known for their usage of makeup, cosmetics and perfumes just as much as their martial prowess. Another name for the hwarang was *hyangdo*, which means "fragrant ones".

In the **Ottoman Empire**, there were multiple layers to the military. At the top were the *janissaries*, the Sultan's elite slave-soldier personal guard. Below the janissaries were the *sipahi*, professional soldiers either given non-hereditary fiefs to govern (*timarli sipahi*) or simply paid regular wages (*kapikulu sipahis*). Below the sipahi were the *yaya* and *akinci*, who were (respectively) volunteer infantry and raider cavalry. The former were either paid regularly, or paid in loot. The latter subsisted off of plunder even when not in military service.

The **Aztec Empire** used a combination of professional soldiers and obliged levies. Notably, every able-bodied male in the empire was required to go through military training just in case it was necessary to call them up. It would be accurate to call this a "levy", although there was a more in-depth culture to it, since training for warriors was intense and started from a young age. The nobility were more dedicated professional warriors, but it was possible for a common soldier to join the nobility (and become a full-time warrior) if they showed sufficient courage on the battlefield.

In medieval **Italy**, the city-states of the region were often very wealthy, but had comparatively low populations. As a result, they relied on contracted mercenary companies known as *condottieri*. Conflict between city states was often conflict between mercenary companies, and as a result the fighting often had low casualties (after all, neither side had any particular incentive to fight hard). Instead, combat between mercenary companies tended to be showy and flashy, but ultimately not particularly intense. In "The Prince", Machiavelli condemned mercenaries as feckless and apathetic, and suggested building a more reliable core of citizen soldiers (who would have loyalty to their home) instead.

In 13th century **Mali**, there was a fusion of sorts between clan organization and feudal organization. The Mali Emperor, or *mansa*, controlled 16 clans, which were headed by nobles called *ton-tigi*, or "quiver masters". These nobles were expected to maintain a force of professional noble horsemen, who were equipped with swords, lances, mail and helmets. Infantry units were levies taken from conquered peoples, and were often equipped with bows and poison-tipped arrows. They were used more rarely than the core cavalry forces.

8.4 Ritualism vs Military Science

Once you know *who's* fighting, and *what* kind of fight it is, you then determine *how* they fight. A culture's approach to combat is based on their goals, their home region, and their available resources. One major consideration is whether the combat is *ritualistic* or *pragmatic* in nature. *Ritualistic* combat is done for the sake of cultural values - it represents manliness, honor, or chivalry in some way. *Pragmatic* combat is purely effective, based on hard military science.

Generally, <u>ritualistic combat</u> needs to exist "independently" of pragmatic combat, which is to say, in a closed environment where it cannot be immediately overtaken by more pragmatic fighting styles. For example, in **Japan**, armies were allowed to fight in a relatively ritualistic way because they were isolated from the outside world, and thus every combatant was playing by roughly the same rules. Combat involved nobles on horse, armed with bows and arrows, challenging each other to individual duels called *ikki-uchi*. Nobles would have their own units of retainers, and "larger" combat was possible, but ikki-uchi were undoubtedly the most important and influential part of Japanese wars at the time.

When the **Mongols** invaded Japan in 1274, they were met by hastily assembled armies of local noblemen with little experience in "real" combat. The Japanese warriors would attempt to challenge Mongolian soldiers to single combat, a concept that naturally meant nothing to the Mongolians. The Japanese did eventually adapt and learn; after the Mongol fleet was thrashed by a typhoon, Japanese warriors snuck aboard the remaining ships at night and effectively engaged the Mongols in close-range combat, which was much more vicious and efficient in nature. Despite the success of this attack, the Japanese swords proved inefficient in close combat. This led Japanese smiths to redesign swords into what would eventually become the iconic *katana*.

Similarly, **Aztec** warfare was based around capturing enemies for purposes of religious sacrifice. As a result, Aztec warriors were highly capable and fit, but fought in a style that was not fully lethal. When

185

they were invaded by **Spanish** *conquistadors*, the Aztecs initially tried to fight in their classic style while the Spaniards fought in a more lethal fashion. However, the Aztecs adapted quickly when it became clear that the Spaniards fought in a different way.

Another ritual/pragmatic split is the difference between pre-*phalanx* **Greek** warfare and warfare after its introduction. In Homer's *Iliad*, combat is described as open fighting between champions, using chariots to carry heroic warriors into battle. Records show that combatants would introduce themselves, make threats, and then finally close for combat. Warriors would open by throwing javelins, and then close into sword-and-shield fighting (this pattern was also used by the **Celts**, **Germanic** peoples, and many other European cultures). This form of warfare allowed for individual bravery and valor, and the winner would often take ownership of the gear of his fallen foe. However, with the introduction of the *phalanx* formation, maneuver and group cohesion became much more important. Individual heroics became largely impossible because warfare depended on everyone staying together, shoulder-to-shoulder, and fulfilling their role as part of the military machine. This is a transition from a ritualistic form of combat to a pragmatic one.

Among the **Anglo-Saxons**, a promise called a *bēot* was made before a battle. It could range from a goal (defeating a certain enemy, obtaining a famous weapon from a foeman) to a handicap (fighting in a certain disadvantageous manner). In the epic of *Beowulf*, the titular hero makes a bēot wherein he says he will fight the monster Grendel without weapons or armor. Completing a bēot granted additional honor and respect for the warrior, but on a tactical scale could be disadvantageous for obvious reasons. As a result, it was clearly connected to a society that saw ritual and honor as being more important than absolute success.

One example of a culture *refusing* to transition from ritualistic to pragmatic is the practice of *counting coup*, which was done by the **Indigenous Peoples of the Great Plains**. Counting coup was essentially a feat of bravery or daring done during a battle. While some of this was practical (recognition for striking an enemy, or stealing enemy equipment), there were aspects of it that were entirely ritualistic in purpose. One example is an accolade for touching an enemy during combat, as in, making contact with one's hand, or a ceremonial stick called a "coup stick". Indigenous warriors continued to do these sorts of acts even as their wars changed from endemic conflicts between tribes to a war of extermination waged by the United States cavalry.

In pre-Islam **Arabia**, fighting was often done between champions at the beginning of a battle. These duels would have a morale effect on the large-scale battle that would follow it. During the Muslim conquests, a special unit called the *Mubarizun* ("Duelists") was used to engage the champions of pagan Arab enemies. At the *Battle of Badr*, one of the most important moments in early Muslim history, combat was opened by a battle between three Muslim champions and three of their enemies, the Qurash. Each of the Muslims won their duel, and the Muslim army went on to carry the day against a much larger enemy force.

A variant of this sort of "champion warfare" was the *bash na bash* used by **Russian** cultures. This was a one-on-one combat (the phrase means "one on one") that would be used in place of larger wars, rather than as a prelude to it. In essence, each side would choose a champion to fight for them. The champions would do battle, and the winner of the fight would essentially be the winner of the battle as a whole. Several such duels are described in *Povest' Vremennyh Let* ("The Tale of Past Years") written by the historian Nestor. Such fights could be between Russian groups, or they could be between a Russian group and a steppe nomad group such as the Pechenegs or Mongols. Similarly, certain parts of **India** used a form of duel called an *ankat* in a similar way, where major political issues would be determined by the winner of a duel.

In short, ritualistic fighting is "knowingly flawed", whereas pragmatic fighting is about ruthlessly exploiting every weakness possible. Ritualistic fighting is about the expression of certain values (honor, strength, bravery), whereas pragmatic fighting is about *winning*. Most militaries throughout history have engaged in combat that falls somewhere between those two points.

When it comes to discussion of pragmatic combat, there are certain concepts and technologies that serve as game-changers in warfare; their development and inclusion means that other armies in the region must radically redesign their militaries in order to deal with them. This is how warfare evolves.

In ancient **Mesopotamia** (specifically, the city-state of Ur), archaeologists have found bodies and ancient copper helmets, which they presume to be lined with linen. These simple helmets provided defense against mace blows; the mace itself was, at that time, the dominant tool of the battlefield. Helmets protected the head enough that a mace-blow to the skull was no longer as sure as it once was, and as a result it is thought that maces were no longer the dominant weapon on the battlefield.

In early organized warfare, the chariot played a crucial role. Chariots began as four-wheeled wagons pulled by horses, but later evolved into a lighter, faster two-wheeled version. Chariots were used across the Eurasian world, from **Britain** to **Greece** to **Egypt** to **Iran** to **India** to **China**. Chariots were often used as a noble-focused form of warfare, wherein a driver would ferry a noble warrior into battle (sometimes duels against other nobles) and extract him if he was overwhelmed. It could also be used as a mobile shooting platform for a warrior to throw javelins or loose arrows while the driver focused on evading enemies. One reason for the early usage of chariots was that the earliest domesticated horses were too small to be ridden effectively in combat, but were useful enough to pull chariots in teams.

The concept of organized shield defenses - whether the **Greek** *phalanx*, **Roman** *testudo*, or **Germanic** shield wall - marked a major difference between organized, well-trained forces and disparate mobs. Maintaining such formations (especially in movement) requires a great deal of coordination and drilling, in comparison with individual skills. Such units were often equipped either with spears, for anti-cavalry defense, or throwing weapons to be hurled before an infantry charge. Specific examples of the latter include the Roman *pilum* javelin and **Frankish** *francisca* axe.

One of the great revolutionary designs that Philip II of **Macedon** (father of Alexander the Great) brought to the world was the *sarissa*, or pike. The sarissa is a great spear between 13 and 20 feet (4-6 meters) long. Like all pikes of similar size, the sarissa was a formation weapon; outside of a formation it was mostly useless. It also could not be used alongside a normal *hoplon* shield, but instead had to be used with two hands, with a light *pelta* shield strapped to the shoulder for some protection. Yet when pushed against other infantry formations, the reach of the sarissa prevented enemy units from closing enough to even do damage. While these pike units were vulnerable in certain ways, Philip II and his successors used light infantry and cavalry to protect their flanks, and the core unit itself remained highly defensible. Ultimately the sarissa was beaten by Roman legionaries, as the generals of the time had become over-reliant on the pike itself without wisely using support units.

While heavy cavalry had existed for centuries beforehand (beginning originally in **Parthia** and **Iran**), the invention of the couched lance made them the definitive aces of the medieval European battlefield. In essence, a couched lance is a lance positioned in such a way that it can be charged into an enemy and make use of the mount's forward momentum. A successful couched lance strike is reliant on the rider remaining mounted (i.e. not falling off), which is why some historians say that the stirrup was the necessary change that allowed for this development. Whether or not that's true is the subject of debate ("The Great Stirrup Controversy"). Regardless of why, the use of the mounted lance charge was vitally important in medieval warfare. The force of a heavy charger plus a couched lance strike was essentially the equivalent of being hit by a car, and knights were capable of charging, wheeling about, and charging again until the enemy lines were broken. Eventually the pike was reintroduced and served as a strong counter against cavalry, especially when combined with archers, crossbows or gunners.

Speaking of ranged units, the development of ranged weapons often created a pragmatic shift of its own. While ranged weapons required protection, usually against cavalry, a long-range weapon capable of penetrating contemporary armor could not be ignored. In ancient **China**, the development of the crossbow (a relatively complex weapon by standards of the era) was used to drive off nomadic invaders. These nomads (such as the **Mongols**) were often armed with powerful "composite bows", built with a combination of wood and horn. Crossbows were used in limited numbers in ancient **Greece** and **Rome**, but did not come into their own in Europe until the middle ages. Eventually they became common across the continent, with the exception of **England**, who preferred the English longbow. The longbow required intensely specific strength training to use properly; the English crown mandated archery training for every able-bodied man in order to ensure a supply of yeoman levies.

It's sometimes said that the introduction of firearms marked the death of the heavily-armored knight. Because firearms could be used by cheaply-trained common soldiers, this is often used as an example of *ritualism* being overwhelmed by industrial *pragmatism*. In reality, firearms and plate armor coexisted for centuries; the first European firearm dates to the 1300s, whereas full plate armor was developed in the early 1400s. Plate armor would often come with a "bullet proof" - an impact site where a firearm had been discharged into the armor. Such a mark was "proof" that the armor was impermeable. Contrary to certain depictions in media, plate armor *did* protect against almost all forms of attack incredibly well, apart from weapons like flanged maces specifically made to target armor. Heavy armor was not truly discarded until the 1700s, and even so, certain cavalry units (such as *cuirassiers*) continued to use them well into the 1900s.

The disuse of heavy armor occurred due to ongoing improvements made to firearms in terms of penetrative power, range and reloading speed. Muskets becoming lighter also allowed the advent of the bayonet, which made the pike superfluous. When muskets were heavier, the pike was needed to protect vulnerable gunners from cavalry. Lighter muskets equipped with bayonets made serviceable spears, and thus could be used to repel cavalry. As a result, the common soldier of the 1700s onwards was an unarmored musketeer, replacing the broader mix of troops from earlier eras.

8.5 Combatant Types & Tactics

The two major axes when discussing troop types are *light/heavy* and *infantry/cavalry*. Each combination has its own benefits and drawbacks, and that will affect whether or not a given culture makes more or less use of that particular troop type. However, a successful military generally makes use of as many troop types as possible, and there are examples of armies that were defeated entirely because they lacked a single one.

Light troops are more mobile than heavy troops, are cheaper, and are often equipped with ranged weapons to allow for harassment and evasion. However, they lack protection, being equipped with light wicker or wooden shields and leather or cloth armor, if anything. *Heavy troops* have an advantage in a straightforward battle, due to superior arms and armor. Heavy soldiers are often equipped with metal armor, such as *maille*, composed of many interlocked rings, or *lamellar*, a linked-together shirt of metal scales. With heavy units, terrain must be used to hem in a light opponent and force them into a direct confrontation.

Infantry are cheaper than cavalry and less resource-intensive. They have an advantage in thick or rough terrain, and are more able to make use of concealment or ambush. However, *cavalry* have an advantage in mobility, and the speed of a proper mount can also give benefits for charging and disrupting infantry formations. In grassland areas (such as the open steppe) the availability of food makes amassing a horse-heavy army relatively simple. Horse-heavy armies are found amongst "horse cultures" such as the **Mongols**, the **Scythians**, the **Parthians**, and the **Huns**. In more barren or rocky areas this is less feasible, and a cavalry-heavy army that attempts to invade these areas may find itself quickly short of food for its mounts.

Light infantry are used for skirmishing, flanking, and ambush. They lack the strength of heavy infantry or the sheer mobility of cavalry. However, they are more maneuverable than heavy infantry, and compared to cavalry they are both cheaper and easier to conceal.

Examples of light infantry include javelin-throwers like the **Irish** *kern* or **Greek** *peltast*, archers, slingers and crossbowmen. Melee troops who lacked armor also count as light infantry, such as the pre-Roman warriors of the **Celt-Iberian** peoples, or most of the warriors of the **Indigenous American peoples**.

At the *Battle of Lechaeum* in 391 BC, a rare matchup occurred: a **Spartan** column of heavy *hoplites* was ambushed by an **Athenian** force comprised solely of *peltasts*. Hoplites were considered the prime mover of Greek warfare at that time, but without faster support, the Spartan soldiers were at the utter mercy of the lightly-armored peltasts. Every time the hoplites charged at the peltasts, the peltasts simply moved away more quickly than the hoplites could keep up. The battle ended with the Spartans fleeing for their ships, pursed viciously by the victorious peltasts. Roughly half of the Spartans were killed before they got away. A similar situation had occurred at the *Battle of Sphacteria* in 425 BC, 30 years earlier. In that case, a group of trapped Spartan hoplites were harassed and ensnared by a more diverse group of Athenian soldiers. The Athenians pinned them in place with their hoplites, then flanked them with javelin-throwers who caught them in a deadly crossfire.

Another example was the *Battle of Agincourt* during the Hundred Years War. In this well-known affair, a force of dismounted heavy **French** infantry was defeated by an **English** army composed mostly of lightly-armored archers. What might have otherwise been a heinous battle for the English was altered by terrain; a muddy field enclosed on both sides by thick forests. Furthermore, the English had dug themselves in with stakes and traps designed to repel cavalry attacks. The impetuous, impatient French knights charged at the English heedless of these risks and soon found them bogged in the thick mud. Arrows rained down on them as they attempted to cross the field; even if an arrow did not penetrate a knight's armor (and it often did), the force of the blow was often enough to deal impact damage and daze the knights. When the French soldiers finally crossed the field, they encountered another problem: they were weary and mud-caked in their heavy armor, while the English longbowmen were fresh and mobile.

English troops (light and heavy) fell upon the dazed French soldiers and dealt heavy damage to them. French reinforcements were mired in the mud and caught up in the first wave attempting to fall back. The result was a messy, brutal battle that resulted in thousands of French losses compared to around a hundred English dead.

Heavy infantry were the dominant combatants for much of history, combining the protection of heavy armor with the relative cheapness and formation warfare of infantry. Some examples include the **Roman** *legionary*, the **Greek** *hoplite*, the **Norse** *huscarl*, and the **Byzantine** *skoutatoi*. **European** knights often fought dismounted for practical reasons (such as the **English** knights at Crecy and Agincourt), and this also qualifies as heavy infantry. The **Iranian** *sparabara*, or "shield bearers", are sometimes described as heavy infantry, despite having lighter armor than their contemporaries. Heavy infantry did best if they were in constrained quarters where their relative slowness would provide less of an obstacle, although against certain opponents in open terrain they could simply power through enemy attacks to engage in melee

A major example of the importance of terrain is the *Battle of Sudoměř*, from the Hussite Wars. The Hussite Wars were religious wars fought in **Bohemia** (the modern Czech Republic) in the early 15th century. It pitted traditional feudal armies against rebelling peasants led by the famed tactician Jan Žižka. At Sudoměř, 400 of those peasants reversed the usual outcome of peasant revolts by standing strong against a knightly army of around 2000 men. They did this with exceptional terrain usage and improvisation. The Hussites used *war wagons*, which were essentially armored carts with ports for gunners to shoot out of, as well as defending contingents of polearm-equipped soldiers. In addition, the Hussite flanks were protected by marshy terrain that proved impassable for heavy cavalry. As a result, the entrenched Hussite infantry was able to resist the attacks of an enemy force that had them technically beat in both quality and quantity.

The *Battle of Watling Street*, in 60 AD, pitted a **Roman** force against a much larger force of indigenous **Britons**. These Britons had already wiped out one legion in the poorly-documented *Battle of Camulodunum*, and saw themselves as poised to destroy a second. The Roman commander at Watling Street set up camp in a narrow area, with high terrain at his sides and a forest at his rear. This meant that the only way the Britons could come at him reliably was from the open front area, which is what they did. Furthermore, the Britons set their baggage trains and non-combatants in a semicircle behind them, which would later prevent their own escape. The lightly-armored Britons threw themselves at the Roman lines, which were mostly comprised of heavily-armored legionaries. The legionaries countered their charge with javelin volleys, and then crushed them in close quarters by virtue of heavier arms and better training. The narrow quarters meant that the Britons were unable to maneuver, flank, or evade the heavy Roman infantry. Ultimately the Britons were routed, but their own non-combatants impeded their escape and they were roundly massacred.

Light cavalry represents the pinnacle of battlefield maneuverability, and was the most common form of cavalry in most eras. Light cavalry was usually equipped with a weapon such as a spear or saber, alongside a ranged weapon such as javelins, bows or crossbows. They were used to harass weaknesses in enemy positions, to make way for a heavy charge or flanking maneuver. Examples include the **Irish** *hobelar*, **Spanish** *jinete*, **Balkan** *stradiot*, and **Hungarian** *hussar*.

The mounted archer in particular was often a dominant figure in warfare on open grasslands or steppe due to their range and mobility. The **Mongols** famously used highly developed horse archery tactics to harass and evade their enemies, attacking when conditions were favorable and withdrawing when they were not. Tactics like these served them well in battles such as the *Battle of Legnica*, a decisive victory against *Christian* forces. Disciplined groups of horse archers, operating with relative independence, were able to outmaneuver and bait the impetuous knights of the Christian coalition.

At the *Battle of Carrhae*, an all-cavalry **Parthian** army defeated a much larger **Roman** invasion force due to advantages in terrain and logistics. A contributing factor was the "Parthian Shot" - a maneuver wherein a horse archer shoots behind him as he rides away. When the Romans sent cavalry units after the Parthian horse archers, the Parthians would evade them, loosing arrows all the while. Once the Roman light units were driven off, the horse archers would resume shooting at the Roman infantry. While the legionary units had heavy armor and large shields, the withering hail of arrows managed to score hits by sheer attrition, and the Romans were essentially unable to do anything about it. Furthermore, the Parthians had one extra advantage: a steady stream of ammunition coming on camel-mounted caravans. As a result, the Romans' only real hope - the Parthians simply running out of arrows - was unlikely. The Romans eventually withdrew in disarray, having suffered one of the greatest defeats in Roman history.

When horse archers were defeated, it was usually in lands that were not favorable to their preferred combat style (i.e. mountainous, heavily forested, or desert regions). One example of this is the *Battle of Ain Jalut*, where **Egyptian** forces needled the Mongols into mountainous terrain and then fell upon them in ambush. Similarly, at the *Battle of Lechfeld* in 955, the army of **East Francia** repulsed a larger **Hungarian** army composed mostly of light, fast units. The Hungarians at that time had been raiding and pillaging East Francia, and Lechfeld represented a rare case where the slower East Francian armies were able to control them. This was accomplished by placing the East Francian army at two key chokepoints: a crossing for the river Lech, and the city of Augsburg. The eager Hungarians crossed the river to attack outlying East Francian units, but soon found themselves unable to maneuver favorably. The heavier East Francians resisted their arrows with shieldwall tactics, then pinned them against the terrain to deliver the killing blow with heavy infantry and cavalry.

Heavy cavalry combines the force and cost of heavy infantry with the mobility and *more* cost of light cavalry. The end result is a mobile, but highly expensive, combatant. Additionally, most heavy cavalry requires extensive horse breeding in order to produce a beast sizable enough to carry an armored rider. Despite these difficulties, heavy cavalry can provide a massive punch in the form of a lance-equipped charge. Some examples of heavy cavalry include the **Iranian** *cataphract*, the **European** *knight*, the **Ottoman** *sipahi*, and **Egyptian** *mamluks*.

During the *Battle of Zama* in 202 BC, a **Roman** army under Scipio Africanus met a **Carthaginian** force under Hannibal Barca. This battle consisted of two major parts: a static infantry line battle and a flank-based cavalry conflict. In short, infantry fought infantry, and cavalry fought cavalry. The Roman and Carthaginian infantry were at a stalemate, but the Roman *cavalry* handily beat the Carthaginian cavalry. When the Roman cavalry returned from routing their Carthaginian counterparts, they were in a position to smash into the rear of the Carthaginian infantry line, causing mass confusion and panic among them.

Similarly, at the *Battle of Issus*, The **Macedonian** King Alexander the Great met the **Iranian** king Darius III. The two sides had set up with a stream in between them, and the ocean on one side. The Iranian armies outnumbered Alexander's, but with careful management the Greeks held the line. When an opening presented itself, Alexander pushed his heavy cavalry through (with himself at their head). Alexander's initial target was Darius, but the Iranian king fled the field. Having broken through the Iranian lines, Alexander turned his heavy cavalry and attacked the rear of the Iranian infantry engaged with his own.

During **Japan**'s Warring States period, the Takeda clan demonstrated the value of spear-wielding samurai cavalry. Before this time, Japanese cavalry were mostly mounted archers. The warlord Takeda Shingen developed the idea of wedge-shaped cavalry formations charging headlong into their foes, which would overwhelm enemies composed largely of foot archers. At the *Battle of Mikatagahara*, for example, Takeda cavalry ran rampant over a smaller infantry force under Tokugawa Ieyasu. However, the Takeda's tactical supremacy did not last long; at the *Battle of Nagashino*, Nobunaga Oda used fortified screens and volley control tactics to allow his entrenched gunner units to bring down the Takeda charge. While often characterized as "new beating old", Nagashino was really more about "new beating slightly less new".

8.6 Signals and Supplies

Raising, equipping and commanding soldiers may be the more glamorous side of military science, but as the saying goes, "an army marches on its stomach". Moving an army has all the problems of moving a town of equivalent size, plus the need for smiths and other equipment handlers, food, ammunition, construction materials for campsites, so on and so forth. In addition, once battle is actually joined, a commander needs methods to instruct the men that can be noticed over loud and often-claustrophobic combat situations.

The issue of logistics is crucial throughout history. Most militaries were accompanied by a *supply train*, a caravan of wagons and pack animals loaded up with necessary materials. The supply train also served as a home to non-combat specialists such as quartermasters, smiths, doctors, and miscellaneous craftsmen. Supply trains were frequently trailed by camp followers, civilians looking for work as tailors, launderers, cooks, and/or prostitutes; these individuals often brought their children along as well. In some cases, the families of soldiers would be camp followers; in other cases, especially in tribal warfare, an entire civilian population would accompany a warband as camp followers.

During battles, supply trains were generally arranged to the rear of the military forces, where they were both kept safe and also accessible if supplies were needed. However, this would sometimes backfire, especially in the aforementioned tribal family scenarios. At the *Battle of Watling Street*, for example, a defeated assembly of **Britons** tried to flee their **Roman** enemies, only to be caught up in their own baggage train and massacred along with many women and children. During the *Battle of Myriokephalon*, a **Byzantine** army was ambushed in a pass by **Turkish** foes, who used their elevated position to attack the supply train in the middle of the Byzantine forces. The damage done to the supply train choked the pass, causing confusion and separating the forward and rear elements.

A partial alternative to the baggage train, at least in the short term, was simply loading each soldier up with as much gear as they could carry and teaching them all the various trades necessary for basic maintenance. This would not eliminate supply trains entirely, but it would reduce their size and thus their vulnerability. This was a principle of the **Roman** *Marian Reforms*; the legionaries, now loaded with 50-60 pounds of equipment each, were nicknamed *muli mariani* (Mules of Marius) as a result.

Baggage trains that accompanied militaries provided immediate supply for those units. However, replenishing supplies and equipment from production centers was also an issue of major importance. In many cases, a military unit would forage food and gear from the surrounding areas. This tendency sometimes led to *scorched earth* policies, where farmland would be burned in order to deny it to an opposing army. For larger amounts of food, and more complex equipment, materials would have to come from friendly territories. The **Romans** built roads across their empire in order to facilitate movement of troops and materials from other parts of the realm. Disrupting supply trains and baggage trains was a major military tactic, especially by light cavalry and guerilla infantry. Alternately, a *siege* (land) or *blockade* (naval) could be enacted, where transportation regions would be controlled in order to deny the passage of enemy materials. This was often used to starve cities, fortresses, or armies into submission. A military force trapped inside city walls was also helpless to prevent destruction outside of them, which meant that even if the siege was lifted, the army might still have trouble obtaining resources to maintain itself.

During the *Battle of the Baggage* in 737 CE, an **Umayyad Caliphate** army was attacked at a river crossing by riders of the **Turgesh Khaganate**. The Umayyad soldiers retreated across the river in haste and confusion, but managed to secure a camp on the other side. However, the Turgesh crossed after them and circled around them to attack their baggage train. Their attack was successful, but the Turgesh were unable to penetrate the defenses of the main force. Despite this, when the Turgesh eventually withdrew, the Umayyads found themselves unable to continue their campaign and were eventually ambushed more severely. An earlier battle from the same conflict was the 724 CE *Day of Thirst*, where an Umayyad army was harried and harassed by Turgesh riders. Eventually the Umayyads made camp and burned their baggage trains in preparation for a confrontation. This confrontation never came, and the Umayyad army was forced to continue on, now without supplies, until they eventually reached friendly territory.

Centuries later, the Muslim forces were able to make use of this strategy against the **Crusader States** of Jerusalem, Tripoli and Antioch. This was the *Battle of Hattin*, where a massive Christian army was lured away from a safe oasis into the deep desert and ambushed by **Ayyubid** Saracen forces. The Crusaders were caught on an arid plateau with no access to water; they were surrounded and besieged, while the Muslims had a steady supply train coming from their territory. Eventually the demoralized and dehydrated Crusaders were picked apart by the Saracens until they were broken and finished.

The issue of signaling was also an important part of military tactics. It is important to remember that all the combatants in a given battle have only a "man's-eye view" of the situation; that is to say, their view is usually obstructed by other soldiers or terrain. The ability of a commander to see all their forces, and the ability of those forces to receive orders from their commander, is paramount to enacting tactics or strategies.

Couriers were often used by ancient militaries to convey orders from one area of a battle to another. Being human, couriers are the most able to give complex tactical information based on what they witnessed or were assigned to convey. As a result, couriers - or runners - are common throughout history, even up to the modern era. For example, the **Onondaga** marathon runner Cogwagee, known more commonly as Tom Longboat, was used as a dispatch runner during World War 1. The weaknesses of a courier are that they are comparatively slow and that they are also vulnerable (i.e. they can be killed or wounded before the message is delivered).

Visual signifiers required line of sight, but was often easier to establish passively. A unit's affiliation or type could be distinguished at a glance, making it easier to determine battle lines and locations. Battles with poor visual signifiers tended to result in confusion and friendly fire; for example, at the First Battle of Manassas in the American Civil War, the similarity between Union and Confederate flags and uniforms led to units linking up only to realize shortly thereafter that they were enemies.

Standards were a common form of communication, or at the very least unit identification, from early history as well. In the earliest records, the term "vexilloid" is used for military banners and markers that are not flags. Their namesake is the **Roman** *vexillum*, which were small sheets hung like sails from banner-poles. Many cultures used a *standard*, which in that parlance meant a pole with a solid object affixed to the end, sometimes with streamers hanging from it for greater visibility. The **Dacians** used a dragon-themed wind sock called a *draco*, which would produce noises that were intended to strike fear into enemies. Triangular semi-banners and pennants were sometimes attached to the spears of the **Norse** (the *raven banner*), the **Franks**, and the **Normans** (as depicted on the Bayeux Tapestry).

According to Encyclopedia Britannica, the use of true "flags" in war dates back to ancient **India** and/or **China**, dated to at least 660 BCE if not earlier. These flag designs were brought to the west by the **Muslims**, whose dislike for imagery meant that their flags were often blank, with a distinguishing flat color used to represent a given dynasty or caliphate. Eventually they were picked up by the **Europeans**, who matched them to noble heraldry for identification purposes. Flags and standards served a rallying role for an army, and a flag falling in battle would result in confusion and demoralization. Unit flags or heraldic flags could be used to identify specific groups and formations, which was valuable for commanders or officers trying to locate allies and enemies.

Uniforms and *personal signifiers* were also of a visual nature. Uniforms consist of clothing, or articles of clothing, that are worn by an entire unit or faction and can thus distinguish the wearer's allegiance at a glance. In many cases, uniforms would also distinguish rank. Creating a uniform requires a degree of standardization and, in early periods, was often done either for elite units only, or using cheap dyes for mass production. For example, the legions of **Rome** wore red or white tunics under their armor, while the **Iberian** soldiers under Hannibal Barca wore white tunics trimmed with reddish-purple. Surcoats were commonly worn during the medieval era to convey heraldic information. Other, similar garments were described earlier in Chapter 6.2. Many armies did not bother with full uniforms, instead settling for smaller common signifiers such as plumes, ribbons, sashes, cockades, or sprigs of foliage (such as the **Welsh** leek, worn by the followers of Saint David). During the Warring States period, **Japanese** soldiers (both common and noble) wore personal flags called *sashimono*, emblazoned with the heraldry of their lord. Japanese officers would also have distinctive crests, horns or symbols on their helmets that made them identifiable during battle. During the Boshin War of 1867-68, certain units on the Imperial side wore long, shaggy wigs called *haguma*, which gave them a distinctive appearance.

Shields were commonly used to convey either military affiliation or personal identity. For example, according to the **Roman** administrative record *Notitia Dignitatum*, each cohort of the army was given a distinct and unique shield symbol so that units could be distinguished from one another in battle. On the other end, a shield could represent an individual; according to Plutarch, the **Athenian** statesman Alcibiades carried a golden shield bearing an image of Eros, the god of love, carrying a thunderbolt. Plutarch states that Alcibiades was despised for carrying such a symbol instead of an ancestral symbol, suggesting that most **Greek** warriors carried a shield related to their lineage or family. The latter pattern may have been common among other peoples.

While flags and standards presented notable visual elements, *musical instruments* such as drums and horns were used for audible elements. Drums and horns could be clearly heard over the clamor of battle, and their beats or notes could be modulated to convey different meanings. In the **Roman** military manual *De Re Militari*, the author describes military music as such: "*the trumpet sounds the charge and the retreat. The cornets are used only to regulate the motions of the colors; the trumpets serve when the soldiers are ordered out to any work without the colors; but in time of action, the trumpets and cornets sound together. The classicum, which is a particular sound of the buccina or horn, is appropriated to the commander-in-chief and is used in the presence of the general, or at the execution of a soldier, as a mark of its being done by his authority.*" Other armies had similar systems, with recognizable patterns used to signal movements that the entire army could hear. In the gunpowder era, the fife (a small woodwind flute) joined the drums and horns in the military musical lineup. The reason for this was that the piercing high-pitched sound of the fife could be heard over the sound of explosions and cannons.

Music could also play an intimidatory purpose, either affecting the morale of enemy soldiers, or by startling and frightening enemy horses. In 684 BCE, in **China**, a battle between two armies (*Qi* and *Lu*) was decided by what was essentially a drum battle. The Qi army beat their drums three times to intimidate their foe. The Lu army did not respond until after the third drum beat, when they charged and overwhelmed the Qi. The Lu strategist, Cao Gui, stated that he had waited until the Qi had essentially "exhausted" their spirits by their prolonged preparation. This event inspired the Chinese proverb *yi gu zuo qi*, "the first drumbeat creates courage" - referencing the initial fervor and energy that the Qi army had displayed. Similarly, accounts from the Crusades describe **Muslim** armies scaring **Christian** horses by the use of their drums; the chronicler Jean de Joinville states that "*these instruments having been invented to astonish and strike dismay; but it is certain that...the use of drums, has originated with the Saracens and Arabians*".

The *whistling arrow* was an arrow whose head was pierced in such a way that, when loosed, would create a loud, piercing whistle. This was used by the **Chinese** and **Mongols** (as well as other nomadic peoples) to coordinate group movements and act as a signal. In **Japan**, the arrow served a different purpose in early eras. Because early Japanese warfare was based primarily on duels between nobles, these arrows were used to signal a challenge from one warrior to another. Information from the Mongol invasion of Japan indicates that the Mongols used bells, drums, horns and shouts to coordinate their advances and retreats - all of which was alien to the Japanese fighting style of that time.

World Cultures

IX. SUMMARY

Thank you for completing this book. Even if it's not absolutely exhaustive, I hope it has exposed you to some new ideas about how societies work, as well as exposing you to the breadth and depth of human expression. An important thing to remember as you move forward is the importance of putting cultural concepts in context. Every major cultural concept is composed of many individual actions and choices. The way an individual acts, or is influenced to act, is an expression of culture. The way a parent teaches a child is cultural, and the way a child interprets those lessons is cultural. Cultural values are subjective and malleable, reinforced through peer pressure and social ties. It must be understood that cultural ideas are not absolute, but merely represent a web of influences on individual behaviors and values. This will not only change the way that you look at the past, it should also change the way you look at our world today.

Selected Reading List

Ford, C. S., & Beach, F. A. (1951). *Patterns of Sexual Behavior*. New York: Harper.

Campbell, J., John, E., & Wormald, P. (1982). *The Anglo-Saxons*. Ithaca, NY: Cornell University Press.

McKissack, P., & McKissack, F. (1994). *The Royal Kingdoms of Ghana, Mali, and Songhay: Life in Medieval Africa*. New York: H. Holt.

Leventon, M. (2008). *What People Wore When: A Complete Illustrated History of Costume From Ancient Times To The Nineteenth Century For Every Level of Society*. New York: St. Martin's Griffin.

Gombrich, E. H. (1995). *The Story of Art*. London: Phaidon Press Limited.

Cook, H. (1993). *Samurai, The Story of a Warrior Tradition*. New York: Sterling Pub. Co.

Shigeru, K. *The Ainu: A Story of Japan's Original People*. Tokyo: Tuttle Publishing.

Gonick, L. (1978). *The Cartoon Histories*. Doubleday & Collins.

Made in the USA
Lexington, KY
16 June 2017